# OSCEOLA

*By R. P. Johnson*

DILLON PRESS
MINNEAPOLIS, MINNESOTA

ON THE COVER:
*"Osceola, the Black Drink, distinguished warrior," from
the George Catlin Collection of Paintings in the U. S.
National Museum.*

Dillon Press, Inc., 500 South Third Street
Minneapolis, Minnesota 55415

Printed in the United States of America


Library of Congress Cataloging in Publication Data

Johnson, Robert Proctor, 1924-
    Osceola.

    (The Story of an American Indian)
    SUMMARY: A biography of the Seminole Chief who was
the guiding spirit and military genius behind the
Second Seminole War, his people's attempt to resist
forcible removal from their land.
    1. Osceola, Seminole Chief, 1804-1838 — Juvenile
literature.   2. Seminole War, 2d, 1835-1842 — Juvenile
literature.   [1. Osceola, Seminole Chief, 1804-1838.
2. Seminole Indians — Biography.   3. Seminole War,
2d, 1835-1842]   I. Title.
E99.S28J64            970.3 [B]   [92]                72-91158.
ISBN 0-87518-055-8

## OSCEOLA

Osceola was the guiding spirit and moving force behind the Second Seminole War. In 1830, when it became the official policy of the U. S. government to move all the Eastern Indians to a new Indian Territory west of the Mississippi, the Seminoles resisted. Under Osceola's leadership, a thousand Seminole warriors held off the entire American army, as well as thousands of volunteers and state militia. During this struggle, Osceola proved himself to be the military genius of his day.

Osceola's story is also a story of the Seminoles: how they viewed the encroachment of white soldiers and settlers, and why they finally decided to resist, against overwhelming odds, removal from their Florida homeland. It is a story of the courage and determination of a people who were willing to fight to keep their freedom and human dignity.

Although Osceola died in 1838, his spirit still lives on in southern Florida. A small band of his followers refused to be moved to the new Indian Territory, and took up a secret and permanent residence in the Everglades. That small band of Seminoles has endured and increased, and their independent spirit has lasted down to the present day, some 130 years after the death of Osceola.

# Contents

# CHAPTER I

# Sign of
# the Dagger

On a stool in the shade of the great live oak tree sat the Indian agent, General Thompson. He wore the full-dress uniform of his rank, but there was little besides his hat and a few tassels and gold buttons to distinguish him from the other white warriors. Facing General Thompson were the Indian chiefs, all wearing the bright colors of earth under sunlight. But the coats and trousers of the white men were of the same dark blue.

In front of General Thompson was a small table, and upon it were a pen, a bowl of ink, and a sheet of paper. Next to the table stood the black man who translated the general's words into the language of the Seminoles.

In answer to the general's command, the Seminole chiefs had stepped over to the little table one by one, taken up the pen, and signed that hated paper. The paper stated that the chief who signed it agreed to leave the Florida territory, give up the land and village of his people, and lead them to a new reservation many days' journey to the west. Now there were only a few chiefs who had not yet signed.

Again the general gave his command in English and again it was repeated by the black man in Muskogee, the language of the Seminoles.

With his eyes narrowed, Osceola watched as yet another chief moved off in the direction of the live oak tree. The name of this chief was Chalo. The white men called him Charley. Chalo in Muskogee was the word for trout, a kind of fish. Osceola did not know the English meaning of Charley, but he did not like the sound of it. To him it was the name of another traitor.

Chalo was tall and straight and he walked proudly. But he was humbled in his heart. Every one of these chiefs, sixteen in all, had been frightened at last into bending to the white man's will. To Osceola, all of them were traitors to the Seminole nation.

The bright April sun in its journey across heaven had spread and lengthened the shadow of the oak tree. In a few steps now Chalo crossed into the dusky shade. First his moccasins and then his leggings turned from a rich pale tan to an ugly brown. Then his robe of brilliant plumage changed to streaks of dismal gray. Finally the edge of the shadow crept up to cover his face. But even the shadow could not hide his shame.

Chalo's face was without expression. Neither custom nor spirit would permit him to reveal his feelings. He was about to perform an act that would destroy his village, herd his people together like cattle, and drive them to a far country. Many would die along the way. It had been the fate of thousands in the past. It would be the fate of thousands more. But few would complain. It was the way of the Indian to conceal his emotions.

Chalo received the pen from General Thompson's hand. Slowly he bent over the small table, lowering the pen to make the mark that was his written name. As before, when the pen touched the paper. Osceola felt the handle of his knife. Again his fingers snapped open as if they had been burned. He clenched his war belt to keep his hand still.

Chalo returned to his place among the other chiefs, and another was ordered to go forward and make his sign. At last all of the chiefs had made their marks on the paper.

Osceola was not as yet a chief, but merely one of the keepers of the peace among the Seminoles. It was a respected position. Micanopy, the chief of the chiefs, had appointed him to this honor because of his strength and skill in the hunt, in sports, and in the war games. Although he was often looked up to as a leader, especially by the younger warriors, he had yet to win the title of chief.

But more and more often, in tribal councils, he had raised his voice in protest against the white man's law. And more and more of the young chiefs had begun to listen to him and to believe in him. Among the Seminole braves as well, both young and old, his popularity had risen like the sun, so rapid was it. This was why General Thompson was afraid of him, and was calling to him now, telling Osceola that he too must sign that evil paper.

Osceola understood the English words but he was careful to ignore them until the black man had said them in Muskogee. Then he looked at the faces of the chiefs. Not one could meet his eye. Their guilt was too heavy. They knew that he accused them of being traitors to their people. He turned and walked toward the fat trunk of the live oak.

General Thompson pulled and twisted the long ends of his black mustache as he watched the approach of this Seminole brave who was not a chief, and yet was more dangerous than any two of them. Osceola wore a bright red jacket. The garters that held up his leggings were the flashiest blue. Most unusual were the two ostrich plumes that stuck from the folds in the cloth of his turban. He was of medium height and rather thin, but in his movements were all the natural grace and ruthless confidence of the huge king of beasts. And when he came near, the way his expression changed from such a depth of sadness to such a depth of hatred made it impossible for anyone who saw him only this once ever to forget him.

Suddenly the steel blade of Osceola's knife appeared from under his war belt. The knife was in his hand and his hand was thrust forward over the table.

"Osceola's sign!" he cried, and plunged the point of the knife through the paper and into the wood top of the table. Then with a sharp twist he pulled the knife blade free of the table top and stabbed it back into the sheath beneath the war belt. He straightened up and looked into the shocked and angry face of the Indian agent.

"That sign and no other," he said, and swung about and stalked off across the ground. Everywhere was a dead silence but for the soft quick tread of his moccasins.

The village where Osceola lived was like most other Seminole villages. All around it were open fields for planting maize. Closer in were the vegetable gardens. The Seminoles were farmers. They owned herds of cattle, droves of pigs, and flocks of chickens. At one time they had been expert horsemen. But when the white men staked out this reservation, they left the Indians only a poor land of forests, swamps, and rivers, where horses were of little use. The Seminoles now used dugout canoes for transportation.

*Osceola, Seminole leader*

On their new land, the Indians cleared away the brush and small trees of the forests with their stone axes and felled the big trees by surrounding the base of the trunks with burning logs. They tilled the soil with wooden hoes and planted sugar cane, pumpkins, beans, and sweet potatoes. Their most important crop was maize, which the white men called Indian corn.

But now the white men were demanding this land as well, poor as it was. It seemed as though they were never satisfied. All along the borders of the reservation white settlers waited impatiently for their government to drive the Seminoles away. Sometimes they tried to frighten the Indians off the land by crossing the border and setting fire to the Indian villages. Then a band of young Seminole warriors would return the visit and steal the white man's food supplies.

Soldiers of the United States army had been sent to keep peace between the Indians and the white men and see that justice was done. Even then, when a white man killed an Indian, he was imprisoned for a night. But if a white man died from the wound of an arrow, the Indian was hunted down and hanged.

And yet the Seminole chiefs had managed to keep the peace. As Osceola walked through the center of his village, he passed a long thin post which had been driven into the ground. The post was painted white and tied to its top was a white cloth. This meant that the village was at peace. When a village declared war, its people tied a red flag to a red post.

Like most Seminole customs and beliefs, the tradition of showing white for peace and red for war came from the Creek Indians of Georgia. The Seminole and Creek ways of life were similar, for nearly every Seminole had once been a Creek or was now the son or daughter of Creek parents.

Until the outbreak of the American Revolution in 1775, when the Colonies went to war to gain their freedom from England, there was no Indian tribe called Seminole. There were only a few Creeks who had left their homes in Georgia and moved south to the Spanish colony of Florida. These Indians were called Seminole, from the Muskogee word for anyone who had separated from his homeland, but they were as yet too few in number to form a nation.

When the war started, both the English and the Americans sent men to persuade the Creeks living in Georgia to fight on their side. The manners of these men were as smooth as bear grease and they came with promises of help and protection, and with gifts of rifles and whiskey. Some of the Creeks were persuaded to side with the Americans and some to join the British. Because of the Creek tradition of using white and red as signs for peace and war, those who fought with the army of the Colonies became known as White Sticks, for they were at peace with the Americans. Those at war with the Americans were called Red Sticks.

When the British were defeated and the Colonies became the independent nation of the United States, the Creek territory in Georgia began to swarm with Americans in search of free land. Most of them were farmers, but many came to take possession of the land for no purpose but to sell it to other white men for profit.

The Creeks struggled to save their homes, but in time they were driven from their land. Even the White Sticks lost their farms to the white settlers. They were at peace with the Americans, but their villages were burned, the men were murdered, and the women and children were forced to seek the shelter of army stockades.

The Red Sticks made no peace with the white men. Their villages were the first to brighten the dark night with the white man's fire. Their crops were the first to be destroyed, and their cattle were the first to be slaughtered. But they did not surrender.

They moved on to new ground, building new villages and a new way of life. While before their custom was to build solid, permanent houses of heavy logs, they now learned to construct the chickee, a small house with a frame of saplings and a roof of palmetto leaves. In this way they

*Three chickees photographed by*
*Frank A. Robinson in about 1917.*

did not lose much labor when the white men came again with their flaming torches.

In one of these villages of Red Sticks, on the Tallapoosa River in Georgia, Osceola was born. The year of his birth, by the white man's count of the years, was about 1803. He lived here with his mother and his stepfather, a white man named William Powell, until he reached the age of ten summers.

During these years, the clashes between the Indians and the whites had been growing more frequent and more brutal. Then, on March 27, 1814, at Horseshoe Bend, the white warriors and the Indian braves met in a mighty conflict. One of the American leaders in the battle was General Andrew Jackson. Fifteen years later, he was to be chosen by the white men as their chief. They called him their president, and they told the Indians that he was their great white father. But the Indians did not accept Andrew Jackson, for none of them could forget the Battle of Horseshoe Bend, where nearly a thousand Red Sticks had fought, but less than a hundred had survived.

After Jackson's victory at Horseshoe Bend, his army overran the Creek territory. General Jackson forced the Creeks to give up all but a little of the poorest land to the white settlers. So the Red Sticks packed up their belongings and moved south to Florida. Osceola and his mother were among them. Osceola's stepfather had disappeared and was never heard from again.

For forty years before this, families and clans of Red Sticks had been moving south into the Florida peninsula. Florida was then a colony of Spain, and here the Indians were safe from the Americans. The Spanish government permitted them to settle wherever they chose. Much of the region was swamp and forest, but more of the land was rich for growing, and for many years the Indians had peace and plenty. Their villages were scattered, but the people visited together and helped one another when help was needed. In time they formed the one nation known as the Seminole.

They became a settled people, like their ancestors among the Creeks. They lived in peace and died in the villages where their fathers lay buried. And they wished for their children to do the same.

But again Andrew Jackson led a military action against them. He invaded Florida with his army. He said that he came to hunt for slaves who had escaped from American plantations. But his main purpose was to force Spain to sell the territory to the United States. This was in 1818, when Osceola was fifteen, and he remembered it well.

Spain agreed to sell her colony of Florida, but first the Spanish chiefs made the Americans promise that no harm would come to the Seminoles. In 1821 Andrew Jackson was appointed governor of Florida, and only two years later the Treaty of Moultrie Creek was drawn up. This treaty moved the Seminoles from their prosperous farms in the coastal regions, gave the farms to white settlers, and confined the Indians in central Florida, on a reservation made up of the poorest land in Florida.

Another part of the Treaty of Moultrie Creek was a solemn promise that the boundaries of the reservation would never be violated. No white man was ever to cross the border without permission from the Seminoles.

But in 1829 Andrew Jackson was chosen by the white

men to become the chief of the United States. And the very next year he persuaded his government in Washington to pass the law called the Indian Removal Act. The purpose of this law was to rid the Eastern territories and reservations of all Indians, the peaceful Cherokees and friendly Creeks in Georgia as well as the Seminoles in Florida. How many promises the white men had broken!

Finally, in 1832, three years before the year in which this story begins, most of the Seminole chiefs, in the Treaty of Payne's Landing, consented to leave their reservation and lead their people to the Indian Territory west of the Mississippi River. Although most Americans wanted all the land in Florida to be opened for settlement by white men, some had been reluctant to enforce the treaty, so there had been delays.

Now for three years the Seminoles had been expecting to move, and the delay had caused them much suffering. Last year they had not planted their crops because the white leaders had told them they would be leaving the reservation before the time of the harvest. But the season for planting and the season for harvesting had come and gone. Another winter, another year passed. All the food supplies had been used up long ago. The white men had promised to send provisions, but only small quantities had ever reached the Indians. Many had starved to death. The rest managed to stay alive by eating what the hunter and the fisherman could bring in.

After the long delay and the hardship it had caused, most Seminole chiefs no longer felt bound by the Treaty of Payne's Landing. That was why General Thompson, on April 22, 1835, had called them together at Fort King. He had prepared a document which stated that the chiefs were still in agreement with the treaty, and he wanted them to sign it. This was the paper that Osceola had "signed" with the point of his knife.

Word of Osceola's daring action at Fort King had reached his village long before him. Many braves left their houses to watch him pass on the street, but none spoke to him. There was a look in his dark eyes, sorrowful, yet full of hate, that warned them away.

A man of Osceola's position in the community had four buildings for his residence. One was a small, snug winter house, which also served as the kitchen in all seasons. Another was built without walls for relief from the summer heat. The two remaining buildings were storage sheds, one for food, which was empty now, and one for weapons, for spare clothing and bedding, and for deerskins and other items of trade. The buildings were framed with poles and roofed and sided with palm leaves. They were arranged so that their back walls were to the Four Winds and their front walls enclosed a square of ground.

In his yard Osceola's two small children were at play. It cheered him to hear their laughter, but of course not so much as a twitch of a muscle let them know it. And the instant they saw him, they stopped laughing and sat there on their heels with their backs straight and their faces without the slightest trace of emotion.

Osceola started into the house. He paused in the doorway. His children had learned their lesson well, he thought. They were very young and yet neither one had shown the least sign that he was happy to see his father. Osceola

*Map by R. P. Johnson*

decided to reward them. Turning in the doorway, he lifted both hands into the air and then raised his voice in a mighty joyful whoop. At once his children exploded into happy activity. Free to express their feelings, they became wild with merriment. In no time they had taken a grip on each other and had tumbled to the ground in a wrestle hold, partly for the fun of it but mostly to show off to their father.

Osceola soon brought an end to this form of enjoyment. He could not stay to watch them. There was no time for such amusements. He went on into the house. He removed his red jacket, his moccasins and leggings, and the turban with the ostrich plumes. At home in his village, a man wore only his breechcloth.

Two women worked in the cooking house. Both were members of Osceola's household. There were more Seminole women than men. When a baby died, it was more often a boy than a girl. And the young men were killed on the warpath. Therefore, if a man could afford to raise two families, the village expected him to take a second wife.

Osceola's new wife was the beautiful Morning Dew. She had been named for the sparkling freshness that greeted the first light of the new day. Her skin was dark like the first shadows of dawn. And to all she was as sweet and full of song as the forest when it awakens after the night.

She was dressed in the Seminole fashion. Her calico gown clothed her from chin to toes. To give it color and brightness, patterned squares of cloth had been sewn to the plain cotton material of the dress.

Around her neck Morning Dew wore strings of beads and shells. Because she was still young, she had few necklaces. As she grew older, the amount of her jewelry would increase. She had combed her long black hair up from the back of her neck and forward over her head, and then wrapped it around a thin flat wooden framework. To hold the framework in place she tucked in the ends of the hair and arranged the hair carefully so that none of the framework underneath would show. What did show was a flat wing of black hair standing out from the top of her forehead, tipped to one side but still shading her eyes from the sun. It was a hair style most pleasing to her husband.

Morning Dew was busy grinding maize. She pushed the round thick end of a smooth stick down into the big wooden bowl to crush the kernels of grain. She was preparing a fresh supply of sofkee, a broth of maize flour boiled in water. The Seminoles did not drink water, only the sofkee. In every village a kettle of the broth always hung over the fire, ready and hot for anyone, stranger as well as friend, who wanted it.

Osceola rested his eyes on this quiet happy family scene. If only it could remain so! But it was threatened now. His family and his entire village could be made to suffer for his bold act in front of General Thompson at Fort King. How was he to protect them?

When Osceola felt troubled, he would leave the women and children and sit alone with his thoughts. Days would pass and he would see no one. Then one day he would make a round of the village and visit all the warriors. He was good company then. He spoke in a gentle voice to everyone, and yet his manners were those of a proud and powerful chief. The young braves were grateful that Osceola took notice of them. Had he wished them to do so, they would have followed him to the home of the Four Winds.

CHAPTER II

# Vow of
# Vengeance

One day news came to Osceola's village from
Fort King. General Thompson, the Indian agent, had forbidden the Seminoles to purchase or trade for ammunition
for their rifles. As a single man, all the village turned to
Osceola to learn what this could mean. Without lead for
bullets and powder to propel them, how were they to live?
How would they kill all the deer that they needed? The
spear and the bow and arrow could never provide enough
meat.

Osceola presented to them a face of stone. "And so once
more," he said, "the white man has broken faith with the
Seminole nation. Once more he has taken back what he
had given. How do the white brothers live together in
peace, when it is so easy for them to break a promise?"

A message came from Micanopy, head of the Seminole
nation. All the Seminole chiefs were summoned to a council.

The villages were widely scattered and it was many days
before all of the chiefs, each with a band of his most trusted
warriors, were assembled in the large round reception hall
of the chief of the chiefs. Benches stood in a half circle
along the wall. These were for the chiefs, with Micanopy
occupying the center bench. The braves sat on the ground.

Since this was a serious and official occasion, the lesser chiefs wore a large ring of red paint around one eye, a ring of black paint around the other. As for Micanopy, from forehead to chin his face had been completely painted over, one half in red, the other half in black. His headdress was a tall crown of the long white feathers of the swan. And in spite of the shortage of food, Micanopy had managed to put on much weight.

He opened the discussion with the hope that everyone would remain calm. Immediately a young chief jumped to his feet.

"Would the white man starve us all?" he cried. "Then let this be a declaration of war."

Micanopy advised them to wait for an explanation from the Indian agent. Perhaps General Thompson intended to distribute food and provisions to the villages. In that case, they would have no more use for the rifles.

But how were the Seminoles to protect themselves, the young chief wanted to know. With no fear of the rifle, the white settlers would invade their land and burn their villages. The borders of the reservation were too long for the white soldiers to guard them.

Chalo asked to speak next, pointing out that since they would be leaving the reservation soon, what did it matter if the settlers invaded their land?

The young chief said with scorn that although Chalo was named for a fish, he talked like a frightened old mother crow. He called on Osceola to answer that squawking old crow, Chalo. At once the young chiefs and braves set up a clamor, each shouting for the others to be quiet so that Osceola could have his say.

Osceola spoke in a mild tone of voice, but his words were bold in defiance of the chiefs who were willing to retreat before the white man's law, a law that would rob them of their land. Most of these chiefs were older men. No doubt they would be courageous enough in war, said Osceola, but age had wearied and weakened them and made them love sleep more than fighting.

The chiefs who had signed the paper at Fort King cried out in protest at Osceola's words. They were only being realistic, they felt. Their people were starving. In desperation, many had stolen food from the white settlers who lived beyond the border. If this went on, it could only mean worse trouble. The only way to bring relief from the hunger and sickness was to lead their people to the new land in the west.

With an outburst of anger, Osceola startled them into a timid, guilty silence. "Any Seminole who does not resist the white man's law is a traitor," he said. His voice was deep and full and clear. And he was very persuasive, so convinced was he that the Great Spirit entered the hearts of men who were fighting for justice and gave them the strength of twice their numbers.

Micanopy raised his hand to speak. He pointed out to Osceola that the purpose of this meeting was to discuss General Thompson's regulation concerning the ammunition for rifles.

Chalo had been offended by Osceola's scorn. He requested permission to address the council. "Is it not possible," he asked, "that the regulation has been made to punish the entire Seminole nation for the action of one man?"

"And who might that be?" Micanopy demanded to know. "And what was the action?"

"Osceola made his mark at Fort King, not with the point of a pen dipped in ink, but with the point of his knife."

"Then is Osceola to blame? What does he have to say in his defense?"

For a long moment Osceola made no reply. He only stood silently with his dark eyes fixed on Chalo. Then he turned to Micanopy and offered to go at once to Fort King and learn the truth.

"And if Chalo's accusation proves to be true, what then?"

Osceola drew his knife from its sheath beneath his war belt. "This," he said, "is the only sign the white man will ever have from Osceola."

The sun had just given birth to the new day when Osceola with a band of warriors from his village set out on the journey to Fort King. Many of the women followed along to purchase supplies at the trading post near the fort, Morning Dew among them. She was looking forward to the excitement and change of the journey.

The tall skinny trunks and bushy tops of the cabbage palm trees were black against the deep blue sky. Only the faintest gray light touched the grass of the open areas. The swamp, the forest, the grassland — all were filled with voices. The croak of the frog seemed never to cease. Once an alligator gave forth its terrific bellow. The Indian could learn only one thing from the lazy alligator, and that was how to lie as still as a log so that even the sharpest eyes found it next to impossible to discover any life there. In just this way could the warrior escape the eyes of his enemy.

Often a fish broke the surface of the swamp and fell back with a splash. The voices of a thousand birds filled the morning air in a song of happiness that the sun was rising. Slowly the sky began to brighten. Patches of pink and yellow light appeared behind the trees.

How Osceola loved this land! He had been sorry to leave his birthplace in Georgia. Then he had learned to love his new home in northern Florida, until the white men stole those rich farmlands from the Seminoles and herded them together in these forests and swamps. And in time the Indians learned to love even this poor ground.

But again they were being forced to move from their homes. Osceola was saddened by the misery he saw. When he thought of the reasons why his people were so unhappy, his heart was filled with anger. Sometimes his spirit became a tempest that raged against the white man's treachery.

As Osceola and his followers passed villages on the way, they were joined by other warriors and their families. Many of the warriors were black men who had escaped from the plantations in Georgia and Carolina where they had been slaves. The plantation owners had sent bands of white men to search for them, to bind them again in chains and force them to plant and harvest without any benefit from their labor. The white farmers said that these black men were their property. The Seminoles wondered how this could be, since all men were brothers. So the Seminoles refused to tell where they had hidden the black men.

The black men learned the ways and the language of the Seminoles. They married Seminole girls and built houses and planted fields and gardens on their own land, and they raised families in the Seminole villages. The father of Morning Dew had been a black Seminole warrior.

But even if the black men had not learned Seminole ways, they would still have been true Seminoles. For "Seminole" was the Muskogee word for any person who ran away, whatever his reason may be.

The eye of heaven smiled through the branches and moss of the live oaks and the bald cypress trees, flooding the clearings in the forest with sunlight. As Osceola passed

*Seminole family, photographed in 1910.*

through one of these clearings, he looked down and saw that he was walking on his own shadow. It was time to stop for rest and food. When next he saw the rising smoke of cooking fires, he turned in that direction, the long line of his party filing behind him.

This village had been built on a peninsula that reached out into the swamp. Much of its land was marshy. For this reason the maize fields and the vegetable gardens were small, and the planting and harvesting were difficult. Many of its houses were raised on stilts above the swamp water, to keep the floors dry and keep out the water snakes.

As Osceola approached the center of the village, he understood at once that all the young warriors here were prepared to march with him to Fort King. For this village was already in a state of war. The tall post in the middle of the courtyard was painted red and from its top hung a bright red cloth.

First the travelers must satisfy their thirst. They passed the wooden spoon around from hand to hand, each dipping from the kettle of sofkee. Then they turned to a large pot of hot venison stew, and the women of the village served maize biscuits that had been fried in grease. The guests were treated to every courtesy. It was a Seminole custom to welcome all travelers with generosity and kindness.

The shadow of the red post lengthened as Osceola's party rested after their meal, until it was time to continue on their journey to Fort King. When they left the village, the number of warriors had risen to more than thirty.

On the hill in the distance rose the high log walls of Fort King. The logs were as thick as a man's body and as straight as spears. They had been stripped of their bark and chopped to a sharp point at one end. Set upright and fastened together, with those dangerous points to the sky, they formed a solid protection for the inhabitants of the fort. The red, white, and blue flag of the white man flew from a tall staff reaching well above the walls.

At the foot of the hill, about thirty walking steps apart, stood two log houses. The smaller was the trading post. Around the other lay a wide lawn of trimmed grass. This belonged to the house of the Indian agent, General Thompson. The house served as both his home and his office.

Thompson stood on the platform in front of the door to his office. Beside him were six white warriors with rifles in their hands. The only weapons the Indians had brought with them were the hunting knives in their belts. They had left their own rifles back in their villages. If the Indian agent had forbidden them to purchase gunpowder, he might also decide to take away their rifles.

The general pulled on one of the points of his long black mustache and waited for Osceola to speak.

Osceola said he had come to ask about the rumor spreading among the Seminole villages that Seminoles would no longer be allowed to purchase ammunition for their rifles. One of the black Seminole warriors put Osceola's Muskogee words into the language of the white man.

General Thompson replied that the rumor was true.

Then Osceola asked if the general had made the new regulation to punish all Seminoles because Osceola had drawn his knife in anger before the white men.

Thompson's reply was indirect. "The Seminoles have no more need for the rifle. You can live by planting."

"But for the maize to ripen, the plants must grow taller than a man. Before the sprouts are out of the ground even to the height of a man's finger, our people will be dying of starvation!"

Thompson understood this. He promised to see that it did not happen. He would ask his leaders in Washington to permit the army to feed the Indians with government provisions until the maize was ripe.

But the white leaders had said many times before that they would give food to the Seminoles and yet none was given, Osceola pointed out.

Thompson's explanation for this was that the Seminoles had stolen supplies of grain and vegetables from the white farmers.

Osceola wondered how this could be called stealing. To bring food and the hungry man together, was this not the very purpose of planting and harvesting? The Seminoles would share their food with their white brothers and sisters who had none.

General Thompson explained the difference between giving and stealing. The white man gave food to his hungry neighbor. This was charity. But if he did not wish to give it, and his neighbor took it from him, that was stealing.

This surprised Osceola very much, for did not the white man grow his food on land which he had taken from the Indians? The Indians had not wished to give it. Was this not stealing?

In answer to this, Thompson only repeated that he would ask the government in Washington for permission to provide the Seminoles with food. He was sure that President Jackson would take pity on the Indians and grant the request.

Osceola was doubtful. For twenty years Andrew Jackson had shown nothing but hatred for the Indians. After so long a time, even the Great Spirit could not soften the heart of such a man.

General Thompson warned Osceola to take care. It was not wise for the Indian to speak insultingly of the leader of all the American people and the chief of their army.

But Osceola said he spoke only the truth. Would General Thompson hide the truth, so that none should know the treachery of the white man? Truly, the Seminoles would find more pity in the heart of the bald cypress tree than in the heart of Andrew Jackson.

Thompson's anger turned him pale. But before he could speak, the wife of one of the Seminole braves ran up to Osceola and clutched the sleeve of his red jacket. The woman's face expressed alarm and fear, yet her dark eyes burned with hate. Finally her tongue found the words to explain.

A white man at the trading post, a farmer from Georgia, had seized Morning Dew, claiming that she was his slave and had escaped from his plantation.

Osceola stared a moment, as if the sense of her speech was too difficult for his mind. Then suddenly he snatched his dagger from his war belt and swung about to face the Indian agent.

Thompson seized the hilt of his sword.

"Do you not hear?" Osceola cried. "The white thief would steal the wife of the Seminole!"

"Morning Dew is black," Thompson replied. "The black people are a slave people. If the white man says the girl is his slave, then it must be so."

"But it is only for her beauty that the white man claims her."

"Is Osceola calling the white man a liar?"

"Not only a liar. Worse, and far worse!" With this, Osceola made a threatening gesture with his knife, then spun on his heel and started off toward the trading post.

Thompson snapped an order. Instantly the white warriors surrounded Osceola. The Seminole braves watched the troop of white warriors marching quickly up the hill with Osceola a carefully guarded captive among them. All that was visible of Osceola was his headdress of white ostrich plumes.

The Indians stood as still and silent as the walls of the fort on the hill. The great log gates of the fort swung open, the white warriors and Osceola passed through them, and slowly the gates swung shut again. If Osceola's followers had been armed with their rifles, blood would have been spilled there that day.

Inside the fort, in a small room without windows, Osceola's ankles and wrists were clamped in bands of iron. The bands were linked to four chains and the chains ran to iron rings bolted to logs in the four corners of the room. Osceola said not a word. His face revealed no emotion. And yet to him no other punishment could so deeply shame his body and spirit.

The white warriors completed the task and the last of them filed out of the room. The door, four thick logs bolted together with metal plates, closed with a hard dull sound that seemed to cause the very ground under Osceola's feet to tremble. The large iron bolt in the door gave a firm clack.

When Osceola moved, the clank of the chains made his

heart pound like the beating of war drums. He lowered himself to sit on his heels. The floor was bare ground, cold and damp. The room was darker than the night when the moon and stars did not shine.

In the eye of his mind he saw Morning Dew walking toward him. He spoke to her and she to him, but he could not hear her answer. Then she disappeared. The white man would die for this. If not the guilty white man, then another, many others, ten, twenty, fifty others.

He closed his eyes but opened them again at once. He would not sleep. He would not rest his body, not in chains. After sleep, often the body forgot the pain. Sleep was death to the spirit, and it often killed the fire of anger. Perhaps he would never sleep again, until General Thompson and the white thief had paid for this terrible shame.

For so small a crime, the punishment was very great. The Seminoles believed that a man who had done wrong should suffer a punishment that was equal to his crime. This was their code of justice. Osceola had spoken in anger. His words had been true, yet his anger was wicked. But this punishment of prison and chains was an evil far worse.

He did not sleep the whole night through. Sometimes his feeling would fill him with a passion he could not control and he would burst forth with shouts of hate and cries of vengeance. His voice was strong — indeed he had been named for the power of his voice.

In the morning the white warriors came to release him. The chief of his village had promised Thompson to see that Osceola caused no more trouble.

The bright sunlight stung his eyes, but the blue sky was good to see. He quickly descended the hill and was lost in the friendly darkness of the forest. He moved swiftly, following no path, wishing only to be alone.

Osceola wanted time to recover from his shame, and time to think, to form plans. He had not seen the sun go to its rest, nor had he seen the birth of the new day. This had happened but a very few times in his life. But as surely as the sun did shine upon him now, the white men would suffer the revenge of Seminole justice.

# CHAPTER III

# Death to the Traitor!

Micanopy was tired. His shoulders drooped like those of a man who had spent the day gathering sweet potatoes from his garden, and his eyes were heavy.

The older chiefs entered the reception hall and quietly took their places on the benches to right and left of him. But the younger chiefs and the braves flapped around and cackled like so many hens. All of them seemed to be talking at once. Every Seminole dearly loved a good conversation. He especially loved to hear and to tell an exciting story. The warriors who had gone with Osceola to Fort King were telling the others about the adventure.

Micanopy raised his hand for silence, but nobody paid any attention to him. His hand dropped to his knee. He folded his arms on his huge belly, like a man who had filled a large sack full of sweet potatoes and was now leaning on the sack to rest.

Micanopy closed his eyes, but not to sleep. He was thinking. After a time he opened his eyes and looked around the room. He saw Osceola and beckoned him to step forward. Micanopy's trick was successful. When Osceola stood in front of him, every warrior in the reception hall was as quiet as a hunter with a drawn bow.

Micanopy started by saying he had heard about Osceola's unhappy experience at Fort King and was sorry. But he hoped that Osceola would remember that General Thompson had good reason to be afraid of what Osceola might do. Was not Osceola's anger against the white man often fierce and threatening?

Osceola replied that his hate only answered the white man's hatred. And now the time had come to answer violence with violence. Then Osceola asked Micanopy to remember that Thompson had broken the code of justice. If the words of a man were evil, then he must be punished with words, not with prison and chains.

Micanopy agreed that Osceola had been treated unjustly. But what was to be done? They wanted no more trouble. They must not anger the white leaders and bring more suffering to the people.

But, Osceola demanded, should he do nothing? How then would this wound to his spirit ever heal? And his wife, was he never again to see Morning Dew? Was he to forget the wrong that was being done to her, who was now a slave?

Chief Alligator asked to speak. Everyone turned to him with interest. He was a pleasure to hear. His voice was like music and he could make pictures with words. When he told of the hunt, even the old women believed that they were stalking the deer or the black bear with spears in their hands.

He had never suffered prison and chains except in his imagination. And yet, when he described them now, everyone was blinded by the blackness of the dungeon, shivered on the wet bare ground, heard the sound of the chains, and felt the cold iron on his wrists and ankles. Then

the spirit of the warriors trembled with hatred for this wickedness. The true Seminole believed that it was very wrong to hurt the feelings of any man. How much worse, then, for Osceola, whose spirit had been shamed! Let him heal his wound in his own way, Chief Alligator argued. And many voices were raised in agreement.

Quickly Chief Chalo begged permission to put in a word. In his opinion, Osceola should forget the injury that was done to him. It was a little matter, after all. Osceola was not the first man to spend the night in prison. As for Morning Dew, could he not take another wife? Besides, the chief of his village had promised General Thompson that Osceola would cause no further disturbance.

Here a young brave interrupted to ask if Chalo could remember when the white man had ever kept a promise to the Seminoles.

Chalo ignored him. He begged everyone to be patient. Soon the ships would be ready at Tampa Bay to transport the Seminoles across the Gulf of Mexico to New Orleans. From there they would march northward to the new Indian Territory. As far as Chalo was concerned, the sooner the better. He was eager to see his new homeland.

Angry murmurs buzzed like hornets among the young chiefs and braves. The older men whispered in frightened voices. Their fears were made known by one very old warrior who needed help getting to his feet.

He spoke of the celebration of the green maize, the religious festival of the Busk. Last year the Seminoles had not planted their fields. If they allowed another year of planting and harvest to go by without holding this festival of faith and worship, the good medicine of the Great Spirit would leave the unfaithful Seminoles and never return.

This was true. The old warrior had done well to remind them, and Micanopy thanked him. Yes, they must hold the festival of the Busk this year. Let every village plant the fields with maize. In the meantime, Micanopy said he would send a party of chiefs and braves to Fort King under the leadership of Abraham. He asked Abraham to come forward and receive his instructions.

In size and strength Abraham was a giant. He had been a slave of the white man until his escape to Florida. Now he was a Seminole warrior. To gain his freedom and to save his life, he had studied the ways of men. Thus, in his dealings with them, it was said that he seldom failed to win the advantage. For this reason, he was chosen to go on many of the most important missions to the white men.

On this visit to Fort King, Abraham was to ask the Indian agent to contact his chief in Washington. Micanopy wished to know the conditions under which the Seminoles were to travel to the new land in the west. Could they count on the support and safety of the white man's army? Would the American government supply them with enough food to last until they had harvested their first crops in the new country? Would they be furnished with horses and cattle in the new land? Abraham must receive a favorable answer to each of these questions. Otherwise, Micanopy would be very reluctant to ask his people to leave their homes here in Florida.

Abraham was also to inform General Thompson that Micanopy was very unhappy that so many white men were trespassing on Indian land. This year the Seminoles would plant their fields with maize and they intended to reap the harvest. They wanted no white men coming in the night and destroying their crops.

Abraham was to ask Thompson why the boundaries were not better protected. This was the duty of the white warriors at Fort King and at the other stockades along the borders of the reservation. By the white man's own law, this land still belonged to the Seminoles. Why then did the white settlers act as if the Indians were the invaders and thieves?

The young chiefs and braves began to shout their approval of Micanopy and their encouragement of Abraham. The old chief of the chiefs lifted both his hands into the air. It was time for the meeting of the council to end. Micanopy prayed that the goodness of the Great Spirit would not depart from them, and that every village might reap a harvest of plenty.

The winter passed, and then came the time of planting. The days of labor in the fields also passed, and the sun grew bright and hot. The fields turned green, then yellow, until it was time for the people to prepare for the harvest. It was the middle of the summer, that time of the year called July by the white men. To the Indians, this was the time for the festival of the Busk.

Some villages were still waiting for their maize to ripen. Other villages had already held the ceremony, which was called the Green Corn Dance by the white men. No white man had ever seen this celebration, but all had heard of it and knew it to be one of the most unusual religious ceremonies of all the Indian tribes. The Busk marked the start of the new year for the Seminoles, and it began when the first maize of the year was ready to harvest.

Osceola and his family began to prepare for the festival. First they collected all their old clothing, all the old cooking equipment — the kettles, ladles, serving spoons, and stirring sticks — and all the old furniture, everything that had been used during the past year. These were carried to the open space in the center of the village. The other families did the same. Together they made a single pile of all their old household goods. Then the pile was burned.

After this, all of the fires in the village were put out and the partly burned logs were thrown into the river. Then the empty houses were swept and dusted and the floors were covered with a fresh layer of clean sand. With the beginning of the new year and the passing of the old, the village too must leave the old and begin anew.

Early the next morning the medicine man could be seen making his preparations for the festival. He was followed by his helper. With the leather pouches which contained the medicine and the prayers, he went to the center of the village courtyard. From here he stepped off twenty strong paces in the direction of the rising sun. At this spot his attendant drove a long post into the ground. The medicine man then reached up as far as his arms could stretch and with a leather string tied the pouches on the post. This was an invitation to the Great Spirit to attend the festival and see the faithful Seminoles at their worship.

Later that morning the old men of the village gathered in the courthouse. They were to hear the confessions of all those who had committed a sin or a crime during the past year. The old men listened to each person's account of his wrongdoing and consulted together to decide on the punishment.

One lazy young man had hidden out in the forest during the time of harvest. He had not picked a single ear of maize. He was ordered to pay a fine, but he had no money. The old men then sentenced him to help the women clean the fish and grind the maize for the feast that would be held on the fourth and last day of the festival.

Another young man had tried to force a girl to take him as her husband. She did not wish to marry him, but he refused to take no for an answer. He pestered her until she broke down in tears. Seminole girls and women were very modest and all men and boys were required to respect them. Not to do so was a sin. To injure the self-respect of another man was shameful, but for a man to hurt the feelings of a woman was a terrible wickedness.

Now, anyone who harmed his village or any person in it, such as this young man had, was thought to have something wrong with his mind. By his evil he was only hurting himself, and no one would do this unless his mind were sick. So that he should not infect anyone else with his illness, the young man was ordered to leave the village until after the festival. Then he was to visit the medicine man to be cured.

Next came Osceola, who confessed that he had spoken in anger to the Indian agent, General Thompson. The old men whispered together a moment, then told Osceola that he had already paid for his sin by the punishment he received at the hands of the white man. Let him go in peace and try from now on to control his temper.

The following morning began the period of three days when everyone must control all of his emotions, and his appetite, too. He was to have nothing to eat, and never complain of his hunger, not even to himself in secret. He must feel no anger or love or hatred. In this way he purified his spirit.

When the three days were over, the medicine man appointed the maker of the new fire. It was high praise to be chosen to kindle the sacred fire. The privilege was given only to one who had never offended the Great Spirit and had always treated everybody in the village with loyalty and kindness.

When the fire was blazing, four huge logs were carefully laid on it to form a large cross, each log placed with one end in the fire and the other pointing toward the source of one of the Four Winds. As the burning shortened them, the logs were pushed further into the fire.

Osceola joined the other warriors around this sacred fire. From the ground beneath the fire he scooped out handfuls of ashes and rubbed his body with them. Then he went to the river and washed. He and the other warriors did this again and again, until their bodies were clean.

A pot had been hung over the fire. Taking their instructions from the medicine man, four young girls prepared the Black Drink, a strong tea brewed from the berries of the cassena holly tree. While a young man sang in a loud full voice, the warriors passed the dipper from hand to hand. One by one they drank deeply of the tea until they could hold no more. Then it was released all at once and the ritual was repeated. In this way the inside of the body was cleaned, too.

Because of his fine voice, Osceola had sung at many festivals of the Busk. He had performed so well that his village had begun to call him Asi-yaholo, the Muskogee word for Black Drink singer. The name was soon changed to Osceola, which was much easier to say.

Toward evening they started the feasting and the dancing around the sacred fire. There were dances for the deer and the bear, for the lazy alligator and the poisonous snake, for the wild turkey and the beautiful snowy egret, and even for the tiny tadpole. Thus did the Seminoles express their love and respect for all the creatures of forest, river, and sky.

That evening the medicine man removed the leather pouches from the post and stored them in a safe place. From the Great Spirit they had received the power to do good. In the medicine now was health for the coming year, and the promise of abundance for the next year's harvest. It would protect the village from the fury of the storm, and give the luck that brought the biggest deer within the range of the hunter's rifle. The medicine now possessed the power to control these things over which a man by himself had little or no control.

Osceola returned to his family. From the storage sheds he brought out the new clothing, the new cooking and eating utensils, and the new furniture. Some of the items had been made by hand, others traded for, and still others had been purchased. But none had ever been used until now.

Osceola felt young and clean and free again. Inside and out his body was clean. His spirit was clean; he had forgiven his enemies, and his own sins had been forgiven. His mind was clean, because not once during the festival had he thought of past troubles or wrongs. In thought and feeling he was like a newborn infant. He felt as though he had been born all over again.

The old year was over and the new was beginning. What

the new year would bring, not even the medicine man could tell. But it was starting out as fresh and clean as ever before, and this gave reason to hope for the best.

The yellow moon grew large and fat until it was full and round, then slowly grew smaller each night until it disappeared. This cycle had been repeated three times since the festival, when bad news arrived from Micanopy.

The white man's government in Washington refused to consider the wishes of the Seminoles. First the Indians were to assemble at Tampa Bay. Not one kernel of grain would they receive. Not one white man would lift a hand to aid them. Not one soldier would protect them from the white settlers. As for assistance in the new territory, the white chiefs offered not a single promise. Nor would they listen to another word from the Seminoles until the entire Indian nation had gathered at Tampa Bay to begin the journey to the west. Only then would the white government hear the wishes of Micanopy. There was to be no further discussion. After the next full moon, any Indian who still remained in his village would be removed by force.

Did the white chief Andrew Jackson truly believe that the Seminoles would tremble at his threat and jump to his command? Did he think fear of starvation was greater than love for their homeland, or dread of enemies stronger than loyalty to the graves of their fathers?

Micanopy's messenger also told Osceola's village that General Thompson had ordered the Seminoles to bring their horses and cattle to Fort King. The animals were to be sold. Already Chief Chalo had exchanged his livestock for gold. The people of Chalo's village had been reluctant at first, but Chalo was their chief. He had persuaded them.

The next morning Osceola awoke before the sun. He rolled up his blanket and sleeping mat and stored them above the framework of the wall, under the palm leaves of the roof of his chickee. Soundlessly he stepped through the door and out into the open air. The sky was gray with the first dim light of dawn.

He ran to a house nearby and whistled softly, then on to another, and yet to a third, giving the soft whistle as he passed them. Then he waited at the edge of the village. Soon the other warriors joined him.

They followed like shadows, walking in his tracks. His step was sure. Even in the near darkness, he knew the solid root of the standing tree and that part of the fallen tree which had not yet been decayed by time. On marshy ground his moccasin fell only on dry earth. Crossing the wide stream, his step found the safe support of the firm rock.

Osceola broke into a run and the warriors ran after him. They must move swiftly now, to get to Chalo before he was warned of their coming.

Chalo had camped with his people on the hill near Fort King. When he caught sight of Osceola, he jumped up and started toward the walls of the fort, but he saw that Osceola would reach the gates before him. He made a dash for the woods.

His trail was easy to follow. He was quickly overtaken. They swept down upon him with the sudden fury of a bird of prey. Their weapons tore at him like claws, and brought an end to the traitor's life.

A warrior from Chalo's camp carried the news to Micanopy. The chiefs were sitting in council. When Osceola entered the hall, silence fell. Osceola began to tell the story when Micanopy interrupted him.

"Is Chalo dead?"

"Yes," Osceola replied. "The traitor is dead."

"Has his family been told where his body lies buried?"

Osceola answered, "By now the body of Chalo is buried in the bellies of the vultures."

A shudder of horror passed through the hall. Nothing was worse than that. No torture in life was equal to the suffering of the body without a grave. In time of war, the Seminoles risked their lives to bury their dead.

Micanopy reminded Osceola that Chief Chalo had been a friend of the white leaders. Chalo's violent death informed them that Osceola intended to resist their demands. Did Osceola realize this?

Osceola said that he would let every traitor send Chalo's message to the white men.

Then would Osceola send the children worse hunger and the women more grief?

Osceola then explained what he would advise Micanopy to do. Let the young of the villages bring in the long cypress logs, and let the old men who possessed the fine skill of canoe-making set to work with their burning coals to hollow out the logs. Let the women fan the coals to quicken the fire. Let the men shape the logs with their axes, chisels, and scrapers. Let every woman, child, and old man have a place in one of these canoes. An easy and quick escape to the swamps was the best weapon to serve them.

"Then would Osceola go to war?" Micanopy demanded.

"The spirit of the Seminoles is a raging storm. Let that storm break loose with terrors of thunder blasts and forks of fire! Let the white warrior be driven before the fury of the storm, to know the vengeance of the Seminoles and the justice of the Great Spirit!"

Micanopy turned to the brave from Chalo's village and asked what he wished to do. Which would he avenge — the death of his chief, or the wrongs committed against his nation?

The brave replied that he would join the great warrior Osceola. He was eager to follow him. And he could speak for all the braves of his village. He knew their hearts. They would fight and die for Osceola.

CHAPTER IV

# The Path of
# the Storm

The scout led the way to the edge of the forest. Beyond lay a stretch of grassland. The scout pointed to a hammock, an island of brush and trees. Beyond this hammock the white men were camped.

Yesterday morning the large party of white warriors with a wagon train had left Fort King. The scout had trailed them to discover their purpose. Finally he understood. They were searching a wide area around the fort, looking for the Seminole warriors who had been sent by Osceola to worry the enemy. When the scout had last seen them, they were making camp for the night.

Osceola listened to the scout, then gave his instructions. He would go alone to the hammock. When he was gone for the length of time it would take for a slow fat man — Chief Micanopy, for example — to go and return again, then the warriors were to join him.

Osceola left the forest and crossed the open area of grass. He moved with stooped shoulders and head low and his rifle level in his hand. His arm was crooked to hold the rifle above the tall wet grass. Every few strides he paused to look about him. At last he gained the brush of the hammock without hearing either a shout or a gunshot.

He hurried now. He must learn of any danger before the other warriors followed him. Swiftly he passed through the undergrowth to the other side of the hammock. He dropped to the ground and peered through a cluster of bush stems, scarcely breathing. Only his eyes moved. The camp of the white enemy was within the flight of an arrow from a child's bow.

Some of the soldiers were folding up their tents. Others were tying their bedrolls. On the ground near each soldier was his knapsack, of such a size that it would cover the full

*Palm hammock in the Everglades*

reach and width of the man's back. How it must weigh on him and hinder his movements! The cook was stirring the contents of a great kettle which hung from a tripod over a fire. A second fire, tripod, and kettle were nearby. Behind the cook was a huge wagon with its sideboards removed. Inside the wagon were shelves and hooks for cooking utensils and iron pots and pans, and sacks and boxes and barrels of every type of foodstuffs.

Osceola heard a rustling sound, and knew his followers were entering the hammock. To the right and left of him they fanned out along the row of bushes that faced the white man's camp.

The soldiers began to file past the cook and his two steaming kettles. With one ladle he filled their plates, with another their cups. They walked on idly to the trunk or large branches of a fallen cypress tree. Some moved a little way up a small hill and sat on its gentle slope. Only a few were sitting close to their rifles.

The two white leaders sat on stools at the foot of the small hill. Osceola had seen the older white man at Fort King. His name was Colonel Warren. A white warrior carried their meals over to them. Their horses were browsing some distance away on the opposite side of the camp.

When all of the soldiers had been served the morning meal and were eating, Osceola gave the signal. Instantly fifty powerful voices shattered the morning quiet with the bloodcurdling bellows of fifty maddened bulls.

Plates of food and cups of coffee were hurled to the ground. The soldiers scrambled for their rifles and the officers dashed for their horses. But now the howling Seminoles came thundering down upon them. The white men scattered. They rushed up the wagon-wheel tracks. They scampered over the hill. They scurried like terror-stricken marsh rabbits to hide in the swamp grass.

Half the Indian war party stood guard in a circle, their rifles in readiness. The rest set to work on the supply wagons and the campground. They collected the white men's rifles and boxes of ammunition and ran to the hammock to hide them there. From the wagons they pulled the containers of foodstuffs. They were lifting these upon their backs when one of the braves on guard shouted the warning that another war party of white men was coming along the wagon trail. The Indians dropped their burdens and faced the enemy.

The white leader rode his horse proudly. But the thirty soldiers on foot behind him seemed to lack spirit. Osceola watched closely as they approached. The white chief drew his sword and barked a command. The soldiers shuffled off to form the line of attack. Their heads were bowed, their eyes on the ground.

Osceola called to his companions that there was no need for them to keep an eye out for the signal of retreat. He brought his rifle to his shoulder. The others did the same.

The white chief raised his sword, then lowered the blade sharply, pointing it toward the Indians. Spurring his horse, he cried the order to charge. Fewer than half of his war party obeyed. Of those who did, more than half were cut down by Seminole rifles. The rest turned back. Then all took fright and fled in disorder. Their leader whipped his horse after them, roaring curses at their cowardice.

Eight of the enemy were slain in this action. The Seminole warriors shouldered the spoils of their victory and left the white men to bury their dead.

Osceola sent a runner to Long Swamp to inform Micanopy of their engagement with the two white war parties. They had fought and shamed the white enemy, and not a single brave had been lost or wounded. Then he turned his back on the bloody scene and led his warriors into the dark and hidden depths of the forest.

They stopped at villages along the way. Where they found hunger they left some of the food. Where there was fear of starvation they left much and promised more. Before the war party reached Osceola's village, not so much as one sack of flour remained in their possession.

Word of their success had reached the village. The large quantity of captured provisions had been the subject of much talk. But the people did not question why the warriors had returned with nothing besides the rifles in their hands. To the Seminoles, it was only common sense for those who had more than enough to provide for those who were hungry.

The Seminoles terrified the white inhabitants all over the state of Florida. They drove the white settlers and their families behind the walls of the forts. There was not space to hold them all. Crowds collected outside the gates and demanded protection. The army put up more log walls to shield them against the Indians.

Even the governor of Florida, General Clinch, turned his sugar plantation into a stockade. He named it Fort Drane. The warriors laughed to think that maybe he had built the walls around the buildings of his plantation to protect his money and horses and stores of sugar cane. The white man feared the thief as much as he feared for his life. And the warriors remembered how Osceola had promised them that one day they would occupy the mansion of the governor. It was a daring and thrilling thought.

It was ten days after the attack on Colonel Warren's war party near Fort King when a scout reported that half the Fort King garrison had been transferred to Fort Drane. Osceola received the news calmly, but it made his heart pound with excitement. Now for every two soldiers who had once been under his command, General Thompson had but one.

Osceola called his warriors together to begin another journey to Fort King. He sent runners ahead to the villages on the way so that other warriors could join him. They

*Picture of a Seminole attack,*
*first published in 1837.*

waited outside their villages until Osceola and his party filed by, then took up positions behind the last in line. They were well along the trail when a runner overtook them. He carried a message from Chief Alligator.

A force of more than one hundred soldiers had come from Fort Brooke near Tampa Bay and was marching north to the relief of Fort King. Alligator and Jumper were organizing an attack on them. Micanopy was reluctant, as usual, but he would be persuaded in time. This was an opportunity to injure the enemy seriously. The weariness of the soldiers had made them careless. Their young chief, Major Dade, rode in his saddle like an old man after much feasting.

Alligator urged Osceola to join in the assault. One more journey of the sun and it would be too late. By then the soldiers would be safe behind the walls of Fort King.

Osceola had few words in reply. Time was even more valuable to him now than before, because Alligator's war party might fail to stop the soldiers. Then Fort King would be strong again. Osceola must reach the fort before Major Dade. He might never again have so good a chance to return the hospitality of General Thompson.

He set off running, and the warriors chased their shadows until they caught up with them. Then their shadows followed and lengthened until they were twice the size of the warriors.

Osceola slowed to a walk. In just a few steps the shelter of the trees came to an end. In the clearing beyond was the home of the Indian agent.

Osceola made a sign for the braves to spread out along the edge of the forest. He looked at the sun. It was the time when the white man ate his evening meal. With the light of the sun against them, the windows of Thompson's living quarters shone as gleaming black as swamp water.

It was dusk when Thompson appeared. With him was a young white chief named Lieutenant Smith. Osceola raised his rifle. Just above the end of the barrel he could see Thompson pinching and rolling his long black mustache. Osceola remembered and a hot wave of shame passed over him. The rifle shook in his hands. This also shamed him and the cold grip of hate took hold of him. He steadied his aim.

On the edge of the porch Thompson and Smith paused to fill their pipes with tobacco. Osceola pulled back the hammer of his rifle and pressed the trigger. The explosion signaled the other warriors and twenty more balls of lead struck the bodies of the white men. While the twenty warriors reloaded, twenty more stood waiting with rifles ready for Osceola's next command.

Osceola raised the war cry and leaped out into the clearing. He sent warriors into Thompson's house to look for arms and ammunition and anything else of value. He placed others on guard and led the rest on a run to the trading post.

The keeper of the trading post fired his rifle once with a wild aim, and then the savage blows of flying bullets threw him against the walls, lifeless. The shelves and cupboards were empty. All of the stores had been moved to the fort for safekeeping.

One of the warriors on lookout came in haste to report that the gates of the fort had opened and white warriors were rushing down the hill toward them.

Osceola ran from the cabin. He shouted the call to retreat and the Indians returned to the shades of the forest, fading away like the very shadows of the trees at night. The braves lay hidden in the woods until the coming of darkness, when the soldiers gave up their hunt for them and went back to the fort. Then the Indians made good their escape.

In the fields outside a village they met an old man who was standing guard with bow and arrows. He told them that Chief Alligator had won a great victory for the Seminoles that day. Out of more than a hundred of the white enemy only three had escaped with their lives, and those three had been mortally wounded. The warriors had made camp in Wahoo Swamp and no doubt were still celebrating.

Osceola thanked the old man and hurried on. The news of the victory passed excitedly along the file of warriors behind him. Thoughts of food and rest were forgotten. Everyone was eager to hear the story of the battle against the troops of the white chief, Major Dade.

They reached Wahoo Swamp well before the first light of the sun. Chief Alligator came with outstretched hand to meet Osceola. Their right arms came together and each grasped the other by the arm above the wrist, in the greeting of two Seminole friends. They moved into the light of the nearest campfire. Osceola squatted down close to the fire, setting the stock of his rifle to the ground and holding the barrel with both hands for support. The dancing light and crackling heat of the fire cheered and comforted him.

In the light he could see the faces of the other warriors clearly. All wore smiles and some could not keep from laughing. Others all over the camp were still giving out whoops of triumph. Many of the warriors had broken away into pairs and small groups. Each one wished to tell the story of his adventure, and he had a better chance if he competed with only one or two others.

Osceola asked Chief Alligator if the Seminoles had suffered many losses.

Alligator answered that three braves had gone to the arms of the Great Spirit.

Micanopy had taken part in the campaign too, Alligator continued. Poor Micanopy, he was old and he carried the weight and trouble of a mother black bear with new cubs. It was painful for him to move with any speed, and he could not run at all. Also, he loved his people well and feared to make a mistake that would hurt them. But Jumper had persuaded him at last. And then what a change in the old chief of the chiefs! Even like a boy who had not yet seen the blood of war, he was filled with the spirit of battle. When the attack began, not another Seminole was closer to the enemy than Micanopy. And of course he fired the first shot, the signal for the action to begin.

When the smoke of battle had blown away, the Seminoles were richer by eight horses, four wagons of ammunition and food supplies, and one rifle for every dead white man.

By the white man's count, the year was 1835, during the month called December, three days after their festival of Christmas. That day witnessed the first open hostilities of the conflict that became known as the Second Seminole War. The first war had taken place almost twenty years before, when Andrew Jackson with a war party of three thousand troops invaded Spanish Florida. Now today, by their actions against General Thompson and Major Dade, the Seminoles had openly declared their intention to resist by force the invaders of their homeland.

# CHAPTER V

# Chief of
# the Seminoles

The Seminole warriors did not celebrate their first victory for long. Scouts reported that the enemy was again on the move. Nearly three hundred regular army troops and five hundred of the Florida militia were marching toward the Withlacoochee River. They would reach the river only a short distance from the Seminole camp. The white chiefs were General Call and Colonel Warren, and the chief of the chiefs was General Clinch, governor of Florida.

The warriors sprang to their rifles. They turned from Micanopy now, for the old chief had delayed too often, and looked to Osceola for leadership. Osceola moved among them with words of encouragement. He reminded them of his teaching, to be bold but not careless, cautious but not afraid. Two hundred and fifty Seminole warriors left the camp to oppose an enemy force of eight hundred.

Osceola with a small band hastened ahead. They followed the river, led by the scout who had brought the news. The way was not far; the white men had traveled fast. Already the opposite bank of the river was blue with their uniforms. They had found a canoe, and eight soldiers, two of them pushing with poles, were crossing the river.

Osceola sent the scout back to warn the others. The

scout was to tell them to form a line in the forest along the river to await Osceola's signal. He was to report to Osceola when all the warriors were set for action.

One soldier returned the canoe to the far side of the river, and seven more were transported over. Osceola told one of his band to count the number of soldiers who were carried across. Close to fifty of the enemy had reached the near bank of the river when the scout crept through the undergrowth to where Osceola lay. The full Seminole war party was positioned for the attack.

The canoe came and went and came again, five trips more and then ten. The crowd of soliders increased until everywhere through the trees was the deep blue color of the sky before a storm. When the total mounted past two hundred, but before the Seminoles lost the advantage of numbers, Osceola raised his rifle and fired. One of the soldiers dropped his rifle and sank to the ground beside it.

The Indians stepped from hiding, their rifles level with the eye. The soldiers turned, bringing their rifles into position. From the row of muzzles came little bursts of yellow flame and then faint tapping sounds like busy wood-peckers high in the trees.

Osceola's voice could be heard above the noise and con-fusion of battle, above the yells of command and the cries of pain. His shouts sent the braves now here, now there, wherever there was a break in the enemy's line. He himself tried to enter and widen every opening in the enemy's ranks. Where there was weakness, he put new courage into the hearts of the warriors. Where there was danger, he lent the skill and strength of his arm.

Suddenly he was struck by a sharp blow. His left arm was

wrenched backward and instantly became a dead weight. It felt as though a great burden were bearing it down. Then came the pain. At first it spread slowly but in a moment it swept through his arm and shoulder like a fire in the blood. He put his back to the trunk of a tree and lowered himself to the ground. He laid his rifle aside and lifted his wounded arm across his lap.

The exchange of gunfire had produced a thick screen of smoke between the two lines of battle. For a brief while it interrupted the firing. The wind was light and by the time the smoke cleared away, three cannons had been wheeled up to the edge of the bank on the opposite side of the river. From out of the huge mouths of their barrels burst three flashes of orange flame and three spurts of smoke. Then came the roar of the blasts.

Micanopy came hurrying over to Osceola. The warriors who had gathered around the wounded leader stepped aside to let the old chief through. Micanopy examined the injury and directed the warriors to help Osceola to safety. Then he sounded the retreat. His order was quickly passed along the line of fighting warriors.

Five Seminoles had been killed. Two of them were black warriors from Micanopy's village who had escaped from slavery only a short time before. They had labored in Micanopy's fields and he had known them well. He was very sad to lose them. Of the enemy, four were known dead, and a great many, fifty or more, had been wounded.

Actions were few while Osceola's wound was healing. Small war parties reminded the white men that they were trespassing on Seminole land. The soldiers could not leave the forts to hunt the Indian. The families of the white settlers demanded more protection than mere log walls.

Early in the white man's new year of 1836, a force of two hundred Florida militia came to the aid of the soldiers in the forts. They were looking for the honor of capturing Osceola. The warriors trailed the enemy troops, hindering their movements by a storm of arrows. When the white men reached the village, the only inhabitants they found were the mice in the grain sheds.

One day in the second month of the white man's year, one of Osceola's best scouts came running into the village, his eyes shining from excitement as he made his report.

Many ships had sailed into Tampa Bay. Each had

*Picture of fort at Tampa Bay,
first published in 1837.*

landed more white warriors than had marched with Major Dade. Osceola consulted with the chiefs. Micanopy was the last to join the council. Abraham came with him.

Micanopy sighed and shook his head. Surely now the Seminoles must give way before the strength of the white man. Abraham must go at once and meet with General Gaines, the white chief of this great host of fresh enemy troops. Abraham would inform the general that the Seminole nation was now ready to leave Florida and travel to the new territory. Did Osceola not agree that Micanopy was wise in this decision?

Chief Jumper rose slowly to his feet. He was tall and thin. His face might have been carved in wood, except for his eyes. His eyes were like two sharp daggers that could stab right into the mind and heart of a man and find out exactly what he was thinking and feeling. He could understand the most difficult problem and immediately offer the best solution. The people of his village were never hungry. Every Seminole knew about his night raids on the plantations of the white men. Taking only two or three warriors with him, he would return by morning with food to last from one full moon to the next. He was listened to with respect.

He began by expressing his admiration for good, brave, kindhearted Micanopy. However, the chief of the chiefs was no longer a young warrior. Micanopy had seen many festivals of the Busk, and now his age and his food both weighed on him.

Micanopy interrupted. He did not have to be told that he was fat and lazy. Who knew that better than he?

Jumper excused himself. Micanopy would please remember that Jumper was a man of blunt speech.

Jumper was pardoned. He was a wise chief. He did not love to hear himself talk, which was a weakness of many other Seminoles. Let Jumper speak with words that cut the heart, as long as they opened the mind to wisdom.

Jumper continued. "It is the tradition of the Seminoles to appoint the most able and popular among all the chiefs and warriors to be the leader during a time of emergency."

"Then do you, Jumper, wish that Osceola be appointed the chief of the chiefs?"

"When victory is won, the leadership will return to the village chiefs with Micanopy as the head chief."

"But should I, Micanopy, give my people to a man so hot in the blood as Osceola?"

"Yes, it is true. Osceola does possess a great fire of the spirit, which only death or an evil sickness can quench. But he fears no man and is bold in speech. The other warriors admire him. They hope to learn from him and gain some of his skill and confidence. There is no one to equal him. He is the hope of the Seminole nation."

"Very well," said Micanopy. "Let the young warrior provide the Seminoles with leadership. But I, Micanopy, am first in the hearts of my people and I must remain loyal to their trust. This is my final word. Let the chiefs get on with the business of the moment. What about General Gaines? Of course Osceola thinks the Seminoles should continue to resist. Is this not so?"

Osceola replied that it was so. Let Abraham meet the enemy, but with his rifle, not his words.

Osceola said he understood that there were now three soldiers for every Seminole brave. Yet the Seminoles had the advantage. They chose the time and the place of attack, and the white men never knew where or when. They were taken by surprise. This was a weapon of far greater importance than numbers.

Micanopy raised his hands to heaven. He prayed that the Great Spirit would preserve the gentle hearts of his people in their sufferings and keep them from cruelty and hate.

Over the same route that Major Dade had marched with his hundred soldiers, General Gaines now marched with a hundred troops plus a thousand more. Before the last of them had crossed the Withlacoochee River, the first were digging graves for the bodies of Major Dade and his soldiers in the field where they had fallen.

Osceola allowed the enemy to pass on without incident. His scouts had reported the conditions at Fort King. The fort was crowded with men, women, and children from the surrounding farms and settlements. General Clinch, now in command of the fort, had neither room nor food to spare.

After meeting with Clinch, General Gaines spurred his horse to the rear of his army. He ordered his men to turn about. They must return to Tampa Bay.

Over half of these white soldiers were volunteers from Louisiana. They had joined the war party in hope of adventure. They had tramped day after day, and now received for their pains only boredom and sore feet. The nights were bitter cold and the ground soggy wet, and ahead of them stretched more long days and nights of the same.

Since setting out from Tampa Bay, the white war party had been on the move for nine journeys of the sun. Never did Osceola lose sight of them. When they halted to make camp for the night, he studied the condition of their equipment. He noted the quantities of their supplies. Most carefully of all, he studied the faces of the enemy warriors. When darkness fell, he moved near to their campfires and listened to their conversations.

They spoke most often in sad voices about their homes and families far away. Florida was a strange and lonely country. They hated the ugliness of the black waters of the swamps. They felt trapped in the forest; it was worse than a prison. Prison walls took away a man's freedom, but at least they protected him from the Indians and the animals.

Again they were approaching the Withlacoochee River, this time from the other direction. Food was scarce so hunger was added to their miseries. The soldiers seldom spoke to one another except to grumble. Osceola decided the time had come for the Seminoles to make a stand.

A war party of two hundred braves prepared to stop the advance of this army of over eleven hundred troops. They placed canoes on the bank of the river for a quick getaway. The bank itself served as a shield to protect them while they reloaded their rifles. They lay in wait. The enemy approached, and they met him with a barrage of arrows, spears, and rifle fire.

General Gaines commanded a barricade to be built. Trees were chopped down and stripped of their branches. The logs were hastily thrown together and fastened. For ten days the white men were imprisoned in this feeble shelter.

Each night a soldier tried to slip out of the circle of Seminole warriors. He was immediately captured and brought before Osceola. Every night the answer was the same. The soldier carried a message for General Clinch at Fort King. The provisions at the barricade were low, and the message asked Clinch to offer relief. Every night Osceola returned the messenger to General Gaines behind the barricade.

Then one night a captured soldier begged to be set free to go on to Fort King with his plea for help. His message was not to ask for more rifles, but only for food supplies. The men in the barricade were starving. They were slaughtering their own horses for food. Osceola not only gave the soldier permission to continue on to Fort King — he also gave him the company of a Seminole scout to guide him safely through the Indian lines.

Perhaps now the white men would be willing to talk of peace. And the council sat down together for a discussion of the matter. First they directed the medicine man to prepare a token in praise of Osceola. But Osceola refused the honor, saying the victory belonged to all.

The council was in no hurry to settle with General Gaines. The Seminole women and children were barely surviving in the swamps, freezing, starving, tormented with every known misery, bugs and rats and snakes. Despair and illness had taken many lives. It seemed only fair that the soldiers who were causing this suffering should themselves know fear and hunger and the cold of the winter night.

But in time the council did get around to appointing the members of the peace committee. Jumper and Alligator would represent the authority of the chiefs. Osceola would stand for the unconquerable spirit of the Indian warrior. And Abraham, shrewd observer of the ways of the white man, would speak for the Seminoles.

They dressed in all their finery. Osceola wore his ostrich plumes. The white flag of truce was raised. And the committee walked out proudly to face the humbled enemy.

General Gaines remained in the barricade. A group of lesser chiefs came in his place, led by Captain Hitchcock.

Abraham, the son of a man and woman who had come in bondage from Africa across the ocean, now offered to free the white men from their bondage of fear and starvation, white men who may well have been the sons of the very men who had enslaved his parents.

The Seminoles desired peace, Abraham said. Many braves had been killed, and many more wounded. The people needed the help of the warriors who were still alive and well. The Seminole demands were only two. The white man, soldier and settler, must remove himself from Indian land. That land, after all, was but a small portion of all which was theirs by right, and it had been awarded them by the white man's own treaty.

Secondly, the Seminoles demanded that the white men honor and defend the borders of the reservation. If General Gaines would agree to these demands, and give his solemn promise, then he and his army were free to march on to Tampa Bay, unhindered and in safety.

Captain Hitchcock said he was not authorized to conclude any terms of peace with the Seminoles. His duty was merely to hear their demands. He would report to his commanding officer and then return with the general's reply.

The Indians sat in the shade of a live oak tree and waited. The sun completed its journey across the sky. Then it lay down in its bed for the night. The Seminoles retired to their camps.

The next morning was misty, after a long night of rain. The Seminoles began to move toward the meeting place near the white flag of truce, when suddenly the air burst with wild shouts and rifle fire.

The surprise and confusion of the attack gave Osceola no chance to warn or command the braves, but the retreat was orderly. Every warrior knew his canoe and his position. Osceola turned a quick glance behind him to see that no dead or wounded brave had been left to the fury of the enemy. Then he stepped into his canoe and pushed off. In a moment the last canoe had glided beyond the range of the enemy rifles.

Days later a scout came from a secret meeting with a Seminole spy who worked in the household of a white chief at Fort King. He had learned that the attack, led by General Clinch, was a mistake. General Clinch had not known that the Indians and the white men under General Gaines were discussing terms of peace. The cloudy wet weather had hidden the white flag of truce.

Perhaps it was so; perhaps a mistake had been made. But the white man made many mistakes. And the widow was no less a widow, and the orphan was still an orphan.

# CHAPTER VI

# In League with the Swamp

Chief Jumper could speak only a few words at a time. He had run a far distance and was out of breath. All day long he and his warriors had been scouting the enemy troops. What they had seen of the large number and the movements of the enemy had also taken his breath away.

With the point of his knife Jumper scratched a long straight line on the smooth surface of a cypress log. Then he made another that angled back from the first so that there were two lines coming to a point. In this way, he said, the white warriors had formed their lines of attack and the Seminoles were caught between them. The soldiers were closing on the Indians like the jaws of an alligator on a school of fish.

General Winfield Scott was the cunning white chief. He now commanded the American army in Florida. He had replaced General Gaines, but his army was mightier by far. Never before had so great an enemy force marched into Florida. General Scott was a hero of the war in which the Americans had defeated the British so that they could never again return to the United States without an invitation.

Osceola remembered that second great war between the United States and England. It was called the War of 1812.

And this reminded him of that wise and powerful Indian hero Tecumseh, who had visited the Creek nation when Osceola was a boy of seven. It had been Tecumseh's noble dream to form all the Indian tribes into one nation with their own land and government, a nation separate from the Americans. He had hoped to do this peacefully, but the only way open to them was the warpath. Tecumseh had joined the British army to fight the Americans and was killed in the War of 1812. Osceola thought of Tecumseh and was proud that he and his people were continuing this war for Seminole independence.

"How many white warriors are under the command of General Scott?" Osceola asked Jumper.

"If the number is less than five thousand, then I am a centipede with a hundred arms," Jumper replied.

Osceola scooped up a handful of sand from the river bank. He parted his fingers and the sand fell between them.

"No," he said, "the white warriors are not the jaws of an alligator. Nor are the Seminoles like the fish in the river. The white men are strangers to this land, but to the Seminoles it is home, and we know it by day and by night. We know every track and river, every watery pathway through the swamp. When those two lines of soldiers come together, believing they have trapped the Seminoles between them, they will only find they have closed like fingers on a handful of slippery sand."

Osceola called his warriors together. He told them of his plan and sent runners to every Seminole village and camp to spread the word.

All Seminole people were to hear and follow the advice of the wisest old men. On land they were to be guided by the warrior who could best imitate the cat. On the water, near the enemy, they should let the canoe glide past like the alligator. Let the mothers warn their young to hold their tongues. And let all be ruled by the heart of the hunted animal, whose choices were only two, either silence or death.

They moved by night. All moved in the same direction, toward one of the long arms that was half the army of the white enemy. They set their backs to the last light of the sun. When they met the first light of dawn, they disappeared into the trees and brush, and lay silent during the journey of the sun across heaven.

When the sun went to its bed, the Seminoles left their places of rest. The men pulled their canoes from cover and steadied them for the women and children to take their seats. Then they lifted the long poles and stabbed them to the rocky floor of the stream or the muddy bottom of the swamp, and the canoes moved swiftly off. The water passed beneath with the soft swishing sound of the wind in the leaves. Once the canoe was in motion, keeping up the speed with the pole was easy work, for the underside of the canoe was as smooth as the belly of an alligator.

Osceola organized the Seminole warriors into many war parties, each with about fifteen braves. He directed their actions and led a band of twenty men himself. In the dead of night the war parties stole into the camps of the enemy and looted the supply wagons. They retired again to the forest but kept the enemy in view.

In the morning, discovering their losses, the soldiers shook their fists at the trees and shouted in helpless rage at the cold and silent forest. Then they would be eager to encounter the Indians in the field of war, and their anger hurried them into action. Sighting a warrior, they would give chase in an angry and thoughtless pursuit that carried them into the clutches of an ambush and death.

The white warriors made every attempt to assault the Seminole in his hideaway. But they were defeated by the watchfulness of Osceola and his braves and the carefully chosen scouts who reported on the movements of the white enemy. In this way the enemy used up his food, ammunition, and strength. Then he became discouraged. His days were filled with fear and hate and helplessness. His sleep was filled with nightmares. And he lost heart in the cause for which he was fighting.

One day a wagon driver carelessly ran his heavy supply wagon a little way off the hard track. The wheels sank in the soft ground up to the hubs. The horses were pulled to their knees. He roared in anger, calling the horses Seminoles and savages and lazy worthless beasts. The soldiers put their shoulders to the wagon and pushed, but it was no use. The entire war party was forced to halt.

Perched on a low branch, Osceola gripped tightly with his feet so that his hands were free. He drew the string of his bow to his breast, then past his right shoulder until the string touched his right ear. He sighted through the curtain of Spanish moss. The bowstring gave a little whining whistle, and the arrow shot true to his aim and found the silver button on the coat of a white chief. Such was Osceola's strength that the arrow carried instant death. The white chief bent over in his saddle, then slid from his horse like an alligator rolling from its log.

The soldiers jumped up and stared with searching,

frantic eyes all around at the forest. They saw only the trunks and leaves of the trees and the moss hanging from the branches. Many could not control their fright and ran off screaming into the woods. Some rushed to whatever shelter they could find, behind the horses and beneath the wagons. But most of the soldiers remained sitting against the trees with their arms hanging limp and their hands lying useless in their laps.

In this way the superior strength of the white man's army gradually wasted away. With their weapons of surprise and terror, the small number of Indians became the equal of the enemy's multitude.

Finally every last man, woman, and child of the Seminole nation had passed by night safely through the enemy camps. The two lines of Scott's military force came together. The arms of the giant wrestler closed for a crushing and final defeat of the Indians. Soldier met soldier. Between them was nothing but the riddle of how the Seminoles had escaped.

The Americans now pitched their tents in the swamps of central Florida. And from here to the Atlantic Ocean the Seminole war parties could travel freely. Only a few of the enemy stood armed and ready to oppose them. Important strongholds like Fort Drane and port cities like St. Augustine lay open to attack. From the inland farms, settlements, and towns to the seaports all along the coast, the white people outside the forts were defenseless. They nailed the windows shut and barred the doors and spent days and nights imprisoned by fear. But their imagined fears were much greater than the real danger, for the Seminoles had no quarrel with white women and children.

The old men of the tribe led the Indian women and children into the depths of the swamplands. There in hiding they built new villages. They were careful to choose the most secret locations, but still they placed sentinels around them to give warning if an enemy approached.

At night these sentinels were the old men of the village. How they prayed for peace! Their bones ached for rest. But through the night they kept a firm grip on the spear and their eyes glued on the darkness. In the morning they gave up their positions to the boys who were too young to fight in the war but old enough to stand guard.

As soon as he could draw the bowstring to his cheek, the boy was man enough to join the war party from his village. The old men trained him in the practice of warfare. He learned how to use the trunk of the tree as a shield and the branch as a bed. He was taught how to spy or to aim through leaves or grass. He learned how the silky hanging moss would conceal the warrior as long as he kept the moss between himself and the light of the sun. And when a runner brought news of another encounter with the enemy, the boy would struggle with all his might to draw the bowstring to his cheek. He dreamed that one day his knowledge and skill would win him the glory of fighting with Osceola.

The huge log gates of Fort Drane swung open, and another war party of white men marched out to hunt the Seminoles. They came down the path between two fields of sugar cane. The leader was unhappy. He sat in his saddle like a man who had ridden steadily for many journeys of the sun. The white warriors were less and less eager to meet the Indians.

*Spanish moss in the Everglades*

Behind the trees where the pathway entered the forest, the members of the Seminole war party drew the strings of their bows to their right ears. Osceola carefully judged the distance to the approaching enemy, and when it was right, he uttered the cry of the hawk. The bowstrings answered with their short sharp whimpering sounds.

The white leader clutched at the arrow buried deep in his breast, then tumbled from his horse. Two soldiers of his war party were stopped in their tracks, also slain by arrows from the Seminole bows. The other soldiers flew for cover. They pushed through the stalks of sugar cane with such noise and confusion that Osceola felt some pity for them. It seemed as though the white men would never understand how the creatures of the wilds escaped the eyes of their enemy. The soldiers scurried back behind the walls of the fort.

For the third time Osceola and his warriors stormed the walls of Fort Drane. Again they were driven off, but this last assault rewarded them with many wagons of supplies, seventeen of the finest horses in the white man's army, and five captives.

Not long afterward the Seminoles heard the baying of the bloodhounds. One of their spies inside the walls of Fort Drane reported to them that twenty of these dogs had been brought into Florida from Cuba. Since the sharpest eye could not seek out the Seminole, the bloodhound would smell him out. General Call did indeed mean to keep his promise.

The bloodhounds killed only one warrior, but they attacked many Seminole women and children. They would fasten their teeth and tug and twist violently until their hold tore loose. Then with a snarl they would again sink their teeth into the flesh of the victim. When the horror was over, the human bodies might have been mistaken for the remains of a family of deer after a pack of wolves had finished with them.

Then as quickly as it had come, the baying of the bloodthirsty dogs was heard no more. The explanation for this came from a young white warrior. He passed alone through the gates of Fort Drane, carrying no weapon, only a traveling bag made of cloth.

Never before had a soldier left the fort except as one of a war party. But now here he was, a white man by himself, walking far from the safety of the fort, even entering the woods alone and unarmed. This was very strange. Osceola and his war party trailed him for a short distance, then ran ahead and met him on the path. He dropped his traveling bag and put his hands on his hips.

He said that he had been an officer, one of the chiefs of the white man's army. He had left in disgust because of the bloodhounds. For this and other reasons, many white chiefs were leaving the army. For each soldier who remained, two had decided to return to their homes. Now this young white man had begun his journey to his home in Tennessee. Was he to be made a prisoner of the Seminoles at the very time he was giving up the fight?

Osceola told him not to fear. He was on his way to join his family. That was good. The Seminoles wished to do the same. The white man wanted his children to grow up in freedom and safety and happiness and hold many festivals of Christmas in worship of the Great Spirit, that they might enjoy the abundance of the harvest. Since he wanted this, why did he not want it for all his brothers and their children? This the Seminoles would never understand.

Then Osceola asked about Fort Drane, about the spirit of the soldiers and the comfort of their living conditions.

"And why does the Seminole wish to know? Are you a chief?"

"Yes."

"Your name?"

"Osceola."

"Osceola! The famous Osceola? Is this the spirit of the Seminole War? Is this the Indian chief whose name is cried the country over, whose reputation is second only to that of President Jackson? Your fame has spread to north and south, from east to west. White boys put feathers in their caps and call themselves Osceola. New towns are named Osceola, and òld towns change their names to Osceola.

"You wish to know about Fort Drane? Why not tell of it? There is talk of abandoning the fort. It is only a matter of time. You will learn the truth soon enough."

The young soldier then described conditions within the fort. Horses were dying for lack of food and water. Food was spoiling in the heat. The water was rotten, and the air not fit to breathe. The burning sun, how it sapped the strength and dried up the spirit!

From the swamps and grasslands the mosquitoes came in clouds and swarmed over the walls. The soldiers prayed to be left in peace, but the mosquitoes waged their own war on them, worse than arrows and bullets, descending from the air in a winged army of endless, fearless numbers. Worst of all was the disease called malaria, the wound of the soldier in his battle with the mosquito. At Fort Drane, one man in three was sick with the chills and fever of malaria.

The soldier and the settler were paying for their folly. Their own people were turning against them. Every day more objections were raised against General Call and the army and more speeches were made in sympathy for the Seminoles. There were white men still living who remembered the American War of Independence. These men spoke out in defense of the Indians, who were only fighting for their own homes and freedom. When the white people heard about the bloodhounds, they howled in protest like savage hounds themselves. The dogs were hurried out of the country and back to Cuba. There were many Americans, and more every day, who sided with the Seminoles against the policies of their government.

So, the Indians thought, they need only wait. Why risk the loss of more braves? Why spend their strength and their arrows? The inhabitants were already under an attack far worse than gunfire. Patience would be the weapon of the Seminoles now.

Finally, heat, thirst, hunger, and insects drove the white people from Fort Drane. While Osceola and his warriors watched from their hiding places in a hammock nearby, General Call marched out at the head of the sick, unhappy columns of white troops. The worried white settlers with their frightened families followed close behind.

Before the sun had gone to rest that day, Osceola led a long file of Seminole braves across the governor's fields of sugar cane, on through the gates in the high log walls of the fort, into the banquet hall of the governor's mansion.

It was a time of rejoicing, and Osceola entered into the pleasures of the celebration, but not for long. His mind was alert to both the opportunities and the dangers of the future. He knew how suddenly the smiling face of victory could turn into the black gloom of defeat. His thoughts became active with plans for defense and the means for a swift retreat.

There was other work to be done. The sugar cane in the fields was ready to harvest. The old men, the women, and the children came from their secret villages to help with the cutting and gathering of the crop. The women brought with them the muddy paste made of a special wet earth that was a protection against the mosquito.

Still the celebration went on. Boys and girls sang and danced in the field where soldiers had once drilled with arms. Young athletes competed in ball games and wrestling. There was a feast of fish and deer meat. And the medicine man praised the courage of the warriors and gave thanks for the kindness of the Great Spirit.

Osceola called the warriors away from their amusements to tell them of his plans. On his instructions, they put half their powder and bullets into pouches and tied them all shut, to guard against moisture. Then each warrior took one of the rifles which had been captured from the enemy. They carried these rifles and pouches to the hammock and to the edge of the forest and hid them there. And each warrior showed one woman, his wife or his mother, where his rifle and ammunition were hidden. The spot was marked in the memory alone.

And the morning came, the very day for which all their preparations had been made. The first light of dawn revealed the faces of the enemy. The soldiers were forming a battle line along the edge of the cane fields.

The women and children were ordered to fly to the shelter of the trees and brush. Then the warriors made up their own line of battle. Osceola raised his strong voice in command, the voice that struck fear in the hearts of the enemy.

Now the wind was calm, and the smoke of the rifle fire remained in a thick gray shielding cloud between the two war parties. With this cloud to conceal them, Osceola began to lead his warriors in close to the enemy. But a wind came up, and the shield of smoke was carried away.

Then Osceola with a single column of warriors forced a break in the enemy line. By this time, they were near the trees and the hidden rifles, and the Seminole women entered the battle. They ran out with the loaded rifles and back into the woods with the empty rifles to reload them.

All during the fighting Osceola's cries of command, of praise, and of encouragement were heard above the confusion of battle. His shouting strained his voice, and he inhaled the thick smoke from the guns until his throat was raw and swollen. By evening it was painful for him to speak above a whisper.

Victory would have belonged to the Seminoles that day, but for the skill of the white men who fired the cannon. The heavy, well-aimed blows from this big gun finally drove the warriors into the forest. Although the women and children hampered the retreat, with Osceola's guidance the escape was successful.

Under cover of night a party of braves returned to the field of battle to honor the dead with burial. One warrior killed was a terrible loss, and ten had been slain in this battle.

# CHAPTER VII

# The Flag of Truce Dishonored

Two years of war had been cruel to the Seminole people. Their provisions were low and their clothes were in rags. Experience had taught them how to escape the enemy. An entire village could disappear in a single night. But in their haste the people left behind them many of their belongings, which the white men destroyed. In this way the Seminoles had grown poorer and poorer.

They were starving. Their rags could not protect them from the rain and cold. And with their hunger and exposure to the weather came illness. Less and less could the magic of the medicine man remove the grip of death from the sick.

Osceola himself was sick. His throat was sore and badly swollen. Cool water and the coolness of the night gave him some relief, but during the day the pain and swelling returned.

The sickness had weakened him, so he lacked the strength to lead his warriors. It tortured him to speak, so he could not direct and encourage them. He remained in the village. With the information his scouts brought him he formed new plans.

He accepted the bad news along with the good. He

wanted only the truth, and thought only how to take advantage of it. He learned that the leadership of General Call had also come to a dishonorable end. The government in Washington had named yet another commander to take charge of the American army.

This white chief, General Jesup, did not hurry his troops. He moved with caution. The other generals, greedy for success, had rushed into ambush. But Jesup took care to see that all sides of his army were defended at all times.

As they marched south into Florida, the army built stockades, many of them short distances apart. In these small forts were stored their supplies, ammunition, and horses. Day and night the walls were heavily guarded. The gates were never opened without a body of soldiers standing ready to fill the opening with rifle fire. Jesup was profiting by the mistakes of the commanding generals who had come looking for Osceola before him.

Slowly the enemy approached, nearer and nearer to the camps of the Seminoles. Soldiers in small war parties, like those of the Indians, crept silently through the forests to make surprise assaults on the villages.

The scouts observed that the white men seemed eager and happy in their duty. They worked long and hard constructing the stockades, and laughed and sang at their labor. They had reason enough to be cheerful. The walls protected them and their provisions. They were safe and well-fed. And now the sun smiled bright and warm during the day, and the night was mild. Even the weather had turned against the Seminoles.

Osceola's schemes and the bravery of the warriors still rewarded them with the spoils of war, the enemy's food supplies and ammunition. But the dangers were greater now, and the rewards were fewer.

Jesup's army totaled close to five thousand regular army troops, four thousand volunteers, and almost a thousand Creeks who had been persuaded to fight their Indian brothers in exchange for the white man's whiskey.

And so Osceola was not surprised to learn that Micanopy had consented to the demands of the white man. The old head chief, Alligator, Jumper, and Abraham had met with deep trouble at the hands of the enemy. Many of their women and children had been captured. Large numbers of their warriors had been captured, wounded, and killed. All of them were weary of the fighting and suffering. Now twenty-four large ships rode at anchor in the harbor at Tampa. And Micanopy with all the Seminoles who still followed him were camped within half a sun's journey from Tampa Bay. The old chief of the chiefs had decided that his people had seen enough of war. They would board the ships and sail west to the new land.

Osceola was sorry for his own followers. They too were sick of war. The Great Spirit knew how they had suffered and were suffering still. Perhaps the white men had also wearied of the struggle. Perhaps they would at least discuss the terms of peace. And maybe the white man's government would not object if the Seminoles occupied a narrow region here in central Florida as a reservation. It would be a small price to pay for an end to the pain and the killing.

A runner was dispatched with a message to the white leaders. In a short time he returned with a most welcome reply. The white men were pleased to hear from Osceola and very willing to talk of peace. Let the fighting stop at once. Let them meet as soon as possible in friendliness and hope. Fort Mellon was a convenient place for both sides. If Osceola agreed to this location, let there be no delay. The Seminoles would receive a warm reception and no harm would come to a one of them. All would enjoy perfect freedom and safety.

Three thousand starving and half-naked Seminoles appeared from the forest and swamps. They walked proudly, though many were sick and injured and in need of a helping hand. After making camp in the shadows of the walls of Fort Mellon, they crowded the trading posts. But the little money they had managed to save did not go far, since everyone must share alike and be cared for.

Then one of the white men offered an idea. The Seminoles were hungry, and the soldiers were starved for entertainment. Why not exchange one for the other? And so the Indians painted their faces and performed their dances. They donned their headdresses and demonstrated their skill with the bow and arrow. In thanks for these amusements the white men gave them food.

Osceola suggested a game of lacrosse. This created much interest and excitement. The game was played by almost every Indian tribe from Florida on up the coast to Canada. It was well-known but rarely seen by the white men.

The Seminoles had not been able to play lacrosse for a long time, so almost every warrior wished to enter the game. They competed for the positions. But so many wanted to play, and such a number were skilled in the sport, that the sun traveled seven journeys across heaven before all the players were chosen. Even then the number of players on each team could not be cut below sixty, which was ten or fifteen more players than were usually on a lacrosse team.

A tall warrior measured off the playing field. One goal post was fixed in the ground. Starting from this post, the tall warrior ran in long leaping strides across the level open area. The length of the field was four hundred of these strides, and its width was one hundred.

How the Indians loved a sporting event! All of the Seminoles, the baby in his mother's arms, the old woman with her cane, and everybody in between lined the field to watch the game. On one side of the field sat the Seminole braves and chiefs. The chiefs wore their headdresses of colorful feathers. They were proud of their bright colors and could not understand why the white chiefs wanted to wear coats and hats of such a dull blue color.

The players ran out on the field, each with his stick cut from the tough wood of the hickory tree, with a net at the end of it to catch and throw the leather ball. The members of one team had painted their bodies white.

And so the game began. The ball was passed from player to player down the field, to be aimed and hurled finally to strike the goalpost for a score.

The speed and skill of the running players amazed the white men. The brutal treatment of one team for the other shocked them. Cuts and bruises were common. Bones were broken. But luckily no player was killed, which sometimes happened in contests between much smaller teams.

One day a frightful story spread through the Seminole camp. A group of white settlers and army officers had attacked a village of White Sticks, those Indians who were on friendly terms with the Americans. The warriors of the village had been absent. They had been off fighting with the army of General Jesup. Their women and children had been driven to seek the safety of the swamp. One child had been murdered.

The young chiefs and braves with Osceola asked him what he thought of such treachery. The white men had made war on the helpless women and children of warriors who were friendly to them. How would they deal with the Seminoles, who were their enemies?

Osceola was surprised by the question. Did they think that he had begun to trust the white man? Not at all. Let the warriors keep their rifles and ammunition in a dry and secret place, and their canoes out of sight in the brush beside the swamps and along the river bank. Let them watch and listen and hope for peace but not expect it.

Osceola could speak no more. The swelling in his throat was very painful. The warriors left him to his thoughts. He looked after them as they walked away. So many were young, no more than boys. When the white men lost a soldier, they could easily replace him with another, or with two, or even more. When a Seminole warrior was killed, he was replaced by a boy. And the boys who joined the war parties were younger and younger. Some could not draw the bowstring to the cheek. If the war went on, boys who could not even bend the bow would be called to fight. But they would fight, Osceola knew, for the Seminoles were fighting for their lives and freedom, while the white man fought for plunder. He made war to steal the land. He searched the earth for gold and murdered all who stood in his way. And with his gold he made rings for his fingers and buckles for his belt.

With his wars he stole the land and gave it to the farmer. The land of one farmer would feed an entire Seminole village. The farmer could not care for so much land by himself, and so he must steal the black men from their homes and freedom across the ocean, and keep them in chains by night to work for him in the morning. So that he was able to do these evil deeds, the white man broke his treaties and killed his brothers.

Certain white men began to arrive at Fort Mellon. They passed through the Seminole camp, and when they saw a black warrior, their eyes rested upon him for a long moment. The Seminole chiefs went to the fort and spoke with the white leaders. The leaders had promised the Seminoles that no harm would come to any of them.

The white leaders explained that the visitors were plantation owners who were looking for their property. Yes, the Seminoles knew that. They knew also that they were slave traders, hunting the free black Seminole warrior and his women and children. Again the white men had broken their promise.

Osceola thought of his young wife, Morning Dew, who had been stolen from him, and the desire was strong in him to meet the slave traders with his spear and dagger. But he must think first of his followers.

And so, as the sun went to rest, the old men, the women, and the children began to move slowly toward the shadows of the forest. Some of the warriors, one for each canoe, followed after them. They walked with their heads up, and stopped often as if to speak with one another. They gave the appearance that nothing unusual was taking place in the camp.

Once in the forest, they ran through the trees to their canoes. With a strong push on the long pole they set their canoes in motion, and the Seminoles glided off over the dark water of the swamp.

Osceola with a band of two hundred warriors remained behind to make sure that everyone got away safely. Then they too began to stroll among the campfires and meet together in pairs as if to hold a short conversation. When they moved on again, the direction was always toward the darkness of the trees. They entered the forest alone, but at once joined with the others.

Now they must hurry. In the morning the white men would give chase, and their horses were swift. The stockades along the trail would supply the riders with food and fresh horses. The Seminoles had only the strength of their legs for travel and the wild grape for their food. There was no time to build a fire, no time to spear and cook the fish. The camp of Micanopy was a far distance. They would not see the old chief until the sun had traveled another full journey across heaven. And they must reach him before the white men could stop them.

One of the great cats was tracking the Indians. It could not be seen, and the cougar made no sound, but Osceola knew. The cougar was keeping an eye on them. Without seeming to turn his head, Osceola looked away from the trail. Off there a little way in the green darkness of the forest, the cougar jumped from a low branch of a live oak to the branch of another oak tree farther along.

It was a mighty animal, large and powerful. But it was old and could no longer halt the flight of the deer. Perhaps it had smelled Osceola's sickness, and understood the weakness of the weary Seminoles. Osceola had lost the strength of his voice, but not of his arm. Raising his hand as a signal to halt, he turned and motioned one of the warriors to give him a spear. Then he stepped cautiously forward.

He twisted his body as he drew back his arm. His fingers gripped the spear and then he hurled it forward. The cougar dropped from the low branch to the ground. A warrior ran over and pulled the spear from the dead body. It was a beautiful animal. Its coat was the color of the deer. From its nose to the tip of its tail, it was longer than the height of a warrior, even if he stretched his arms high above his head.

Osceola was suddenly very sick. The swelling in his throat stabbed with pain. It choked him. He waved aside the warriors who came to help him, and sat down on the ground, holding his throat gently between his hands. All at once his throat seemed to burst open, and the pain was violent, but only for a moment. A period of time passed by, and his mind did not know it.

Slowly his thoughts became clear again. His mind awakened, heavy and dull at first, as if he had slept the whole day through. He opened his eyes and looked about him. The sun was bright and the shadows were long. It was still morning. He felt weak, but he told himself that he would soon stand on his feet again and lead his warriors to the camp of the old chief.

Osceola rose to his feet. The pain was gone and his head felt light with relief. He felt strong again, and he wanted to shout again, to roar like an alligator. But he saved his voice. It was not wise to ask too much from luck all at one time. He glanced around at the warriors and then set off along the path, walking at a fast pace.

He had gone only a little way when he broke into a clearing in the forest and surprised a family of white-tailed deer. Away the animals sprang, in their alarm poking their tails up stiff, the undersides of the tails showing like white flags of truce. The deer also were Seminoles. That Muskogee word, Seminole, also described the wildness of the forest animal, for no wild animal could be enslaved and made to live a life that was not free. A Seminole, whether man or animal, took flight when liberty or life was in danger.

Osceola was glad to be on the trail again. After the sickness, he felt as strong as he ever had in his youth. He was a true Seminole again. He began to run, his warriors following behind him.

It was long after dark when they entered the camp of the old chief. Micanopy sat close to a large fire, wrapped in a heavy blanket. He held the blanket tightly around him and clutched it in a fist up under his chin. As he sat down beside Micanopy, Osceola gave the old man a friendly greeting. He was sorry if the chief of the chiefs was suffering from the chill of the night.

Micanopy told one of the women to bring a dipper of sofkee for Osceola. Then he asked if Osceola's presence meant that all of the Seminoles were to sail away from Tampa Bay together.

Osceola thanked the woman for the sofkee and drank from the dipper. The hot liquid burned his throat a little, but then it was soothing. Again Osceola said that he was sorry, this time because the old chief must leave the warmth of his campfire. The Seminoles must continue to resist the white man, because the slave traders were again on the prowl.

"But General Jesup has promised me that no black warrior is to be separated from his family or the tribe," Micanopy protested.

"And why do you think that the word of General Jesup can be trusted?"

Micanopy could give no reason, except to say that he had been sick with the white man's disease called the measles. Many in his camp had also fallen ill with the disease, and all were weary of the fighting. He pointed out that Osceola was sick, too, and his spirit was weak. Without his strong spirit, the Seminoles must give up war against the white man.

"Then is the fate of the black Seminoles to be that of their black brothers from Africa, either slavery or death?" Osceola demanded.

Micanopy was silent. So what more was there for Osceola to say? He jumped to his feet and ordered two warriors to stand guard over Micanopy, should the old chief attempt to escape or interfere with Osceola's plan.

Scouts were sent out to look over the grounds, to judge the distance to the forest and the river, and to find the camps of the white men and the stockades where the Seminole warriors were held prisoner.

When they returned with their reports, Osceola questioned them carefully. Had they marked well in their minds the locations of all gates, the numbers of sentinels, how far the soldiers' quarters were from the cannons? Success required the most careful plans and perfect timing.

Osceola paced to and fro. He could not stand still. He was too eager to know the outcome of this most daring action of all. He wanted to escape with all his prizes or to be captured and have the matter over with.

That night, Osceola led his warriors to battle in the most glorious achievement of all in the long series of attacks and escapes that he had successfully commanded.

Hardly a shot was fired, or a soldier disturbed in his sleep, or a sentry troubled with alarm. Yet it was a most shameful and crushing defeat for the commander of the army, General Jesup, resulting in Osceola's kidnaping of Micanopy and his release of seven hundred Seminole prisoners of war.

The runner came bounding breathlessly into the camp. He stopped within two leaps of Osceola, panting and puffing. He brought greetings from the white chief of the army. General Jesup asked if the great warrior Osceola would consent to meet with the white leaders to discuss a settlement of the disagreement between the Seminole nation and the United States.

So now, was it finally to be? Were the Seminoles to live in peace at last? Were they once again to fly the white flag from the white stick in the village courtyard? Were they once more to see the smiles of the women and hear the laughter of the children?

It was a cheerful party of warriors who shouted farewell to the people of the camp the next morning and started on the journey of good will and friendship with the white man. Their number was fifty, and not a single serious face could be seen among them. They carried their fine clothes in bundles on their backs and wore only their breechcloths. And they walked in peace, out in the open, freely, unafraid, with no hatred in their hearts and no evil in their thoughts.

A flock of spoonbills rose from the surface of the swamp, skimming the water, then turning gracefully and rising up and up toward the blue heavens. With them the spirits of the Seminoles also were lifted to heaven. How free were the birds! How happy the sight of them!

As he walked, Osceola remembered when he was a boy among the Creeks, a free and happy little animal of the forest, running the pathways and climbing high into the tall trees. His house had been so strong that the same Creek family had lived there for three generations.

Now those days, those happy years, were to happen again. Osceola's children could live their early years just as their father had lived his. And so would all the Seminole children grow up to remember the years when they played freely with joyful hearts.

The party of Seminole warriors met the white leaders and soldiers near the old Spanish seaport of St. Augustine on the Atlantic coast. First they dressed in their feathers and leggings and all of their finery. Then they walked out as proud, free men and victorious warriors, to talk with the enemy under the white flag of truce.

And under that white flag, the soldiers were ordered to surround the Seminoles, seize them, and take them captive. Those words of command were the only ones ever spoken under that flag of truce.

The Indians were marched down the main street of St. Augustine. The white people lined the sidewalks to watch them pass. They looked on with curiosity and amusement, as they might have viewed a parade. They did not yet know that General Jesup had dishonored the white flag of truce.

No pledge between two nations, two war parties, two men was more sacred than this. Standing beneath a flag of truce, the worst enemy, however evil his actions, was not to be harmed. How could hatred and killing ever end, if the enemies could not meet safely together to talk of peace? Jesup had broken the highest trust.

The famous and the powerful came to visit Osceola in prison. Head chiefs of other Indian nations came to honor him. The white men praised his courage and his deeds. The Indians tried to comfort him. But who could tell him why the general of the American army had violated the white flag of truce and brought shame to himself and to his country?

*St. Augustine*
*at about the time of the Civil War.*

Jesup had no victory. Instead of the shame of defeat, he chose to dishonor the symbol of peace. Disgrace there was, but his job was done. The spirit of the Seminole War lay sick and dying in an American dungeon.

Imprisoned, the spirit of Osceola died. It was time then for his body to die also. He asked to see his family. They were sad to find that he was ill. They too were pale and thin, from the constant danger and the poverty of the three years of the war. But the young ones were still fine-looking children, with the gentle manners and modesty of proper Seminoles, and he was very proud of them.

To his great joy, his young and beautiful wife, Morning Dew, was again a free woman. When they saw one another, they could hardly keep back the tears. But in front of the children they controlled their emotions, in the Seminole fashion.

On the thirtieth day of the white man's year of 1838, Osceola went to ask the Great Spirit why the white man refused to share the good land with his brothers the Seminoles.

Photo by Robert Wilcox

## THE AUTHOR

R. P. Johnson is a native of Minnesota and a graduate of the University of Minnesota. His early interest was theater, as an actor and playwright. Since then he has written fiction (a novel, *Legacy of Thorns,* appeared in 1965), book reviews, and criticism. Mr. Johnson has also worked as an editor and a historian, and has taught high school in Idaho, Michigan, and Minnesota. In 1971, he received a fellowship from the Edward MacDowell Colony for artists in New Hampshire. He is currently living in Minnesota, occupied with writing and with continued study of his primary interest, literature.

*The photographs are reproduced through the courtesy of the Library of Congress; Smithsonian Institution National Anthropological Archives; State Photographic Archives, Strozier Library, Florida State University; and U. S. Department of the Interior, National Park Service.*

OTHER BIOGRAPHIES
IN THIS SERIES ARE

## DATE DUE

| | | |
|---|---|---|
| MAY 1 3 1983 | | |
| MAY 1 8 1984 | | |
| APR 2 5 1986 | | |
| MAR 2 1 1994 | | |
| | | |
| | | |
| | | |
| | | |
| | | |
| | | |
| | | |
| | | |
| | | |
| | | |
| | | |

HIGHSMITH 45-102                    PRI